IMPROMPTU FRIDAY NIGHTS

Impromptu Friday Nights

A Guide to Supper Clubs

Paul J. Kenny

NEW YORK

NASHVILLE • MELBOURNE • VANCOUVER

Impromptu Friday Nights

A Guide to Supper Clubs

Published in New York, New York, by Morgan James Publishing. Morgan James is a trademark of Morgan James, LLC. www.MorganJamesPublishing.com

The Morgan James Speakers Group can bring authors to your live event. For more information or to book an event visit The Morgan James Speakers Group at www.TheMorganJamesSpeakersGroup.com.

ISBN 9781683505044 - paperback
ISBN 9781683505051 - eBook
Library of Congress Control Number: 2017904092

Cover Design by: Chris Treccani
www.3dogdesign.com

Interior Design by: Paul Curtis

In an effort to support local communities, raise awareness and funds, Morgan James Publishing donates a percentage of all book sales for the life of each book to Habitat for Humanity Peninsula and Greater Williamsburg.

Get involved today! Visit
www.MorganJamesBuilds.com

Table of Contents

Introduction   **3**

Acknowledgments   **5**

Chapter 1: Finding the Right People   **9**
Shrimp and Avocado Quesadillas
Seared Baja Beef Tenderloin
Spring Greens with Mustard/Horseradish Sauce
Endive, Pear and Blue Cheese Salad
Sesame Chilean Sea Bass with Wasabi/Soy Beurre Blanc Sauce
Asparagus and Black Rice
Poached Peaches with Vanilla Ice Cream and Blueberry Compote

Chapter 2: Mise en Place   **13**
Romaine Wedge
Gorgonzola Stuffed Shrimp
Pan Roasted Cod Loin with Sauce Americaine
Green Beans
Rice
Rack of Lamb Provençale with a Béarnaise Blush Sauce
Pommes Frites
Sautéed Asparagus
Carrot Cake and German Chocolate Cake Minis with Grand Marnier infused
Berries and Vanilla Ice Cream

Chapter 3: The Classic Club   **35**
Gorgonzola Enrobed Grapes
Romaine Wedge with Gorgonzola Vinaigrette
Rack of Lamb Provençale
with Cabernet Infused Demi-glace
Pommes Macaire
Sautéed Chanterelles
Haricot Verts with Sautéed Shallot and Pine Nuts
Cookie Balls with Grand Marnier infused Raspberries

Chapter 4: Impromptu Friday Nights   **81**
Crudité with Tapenade
Roasted Red Bell Peppers with Buffalo Mozzarella and Basil Pesto
Chicken Milanese with Salsa Verde
Pasta with Sausage Olive Oil, Garlic and Fresh Herbs
Baked Escarole
Berries in a Grand Marnier Sauce

Chapter 5: The Four Couples Club   **97**
Salami Stuffed with Asparagus and Pesto Cream Cheese
Cheese Puffs with Bacon and Shallot
Mozzarella Stuffed Meatballs with Sweet Chile Sauce
Roasted Beets with Fresh Mozzarella and a Balsamic Reduction
Tomato and Watermelon Salad with Olive Oil and Basil
Char Roasted Garlic Bread with and Arugula Salad
Brussel Sprout Leaves with Caramelized Garlic and Bacon
Spiced Chocolate Honey Mousse

Chapter 6: Send Out the Email   **119**
Antipasti - Salami - Provolone - Olives - White Beans
Lasagna
Grill Roasted Italian Sausages
Chopped Salad with Italian Dressing
Garlic Bread
Grilled Eggplant With Tomato Concassé
Cannoli

Chapter 7: "I Don't Cook, but I Know Where to Buy"   **137**

Hamptons	*Memphis*
Seafood Spread	Spinach, Artichoke, Parmesan Dip
Shallot and Blue Cheese Dip	Chips
Crackers, Crudité and Chips	Teriyaki Pineapple Meatballs
Lobster's	BBQ Ribs
Broccoli Cole Slaw	Beans
Potato Salad	Slaw
Bread and Butter	Rolls
French Lentils with Vinaigrette	Cookies
Berry Pie	Cupcakes
Ice Cream	Ice Cream

Chapter 8: Kickoff Party   **145**
Margherita (Tomato, Fresh Mozzarella and Basil) Grilled Pizzas
Sausage and Mushroom
Sausage and Mushroom
Shrimp and Bacon
White/Broccoli
Wild Mushrooms, Caramelized Onion and Gorgonzola
Meat Lovers with Sausage, Meatball and Bacon
Caramelized Leek and Goat Cheese
Roasted Garlic and Fresh Mozzarella
Clam, Bacon and Mozzarella with Fresh Oregano

Introduction

Just about everyone likes to socialize over a meal. Supper clubs are a great way to bring people together around food. Sounds simple, but like many things, it is easier said than done. There are all kinds of challenges to organizing a supper club:

- How can I find the right people?
- How do I make the idea of entertaining less intimidating?
- Where do I find the time to pull it together?
- How much do I have to clean and set up?
- What if I can't cook?
- Where do I get the recipes?
- How do I organize the food, the delegation and the process?

The purpose of this book is to provide answers to most of these challenges. I will also try to demystify the process with the ultimate goal of making supper clubs simple and fun.

Preparation, or having your mise en place, becomes your security blanket. Above all else, mise en place is the key to addressing the intimidation factor and the other supper club challenges listed above.

There is not one type of supper club. In fact, there are probably dozens of different variations on the same theme. Simply put, a supper club is a way for groups, large or small, formally or informally, to socialize over a meal. This book will take you through five different types of clubs:

1. **The Classic Club.** This is one of the more formal supper clubs and one that we have had in my neighborhood for over 22 years. There is quite a bit of structure in this club, with a club board putting together parings of couples, menus etc.

2. **Impromptu Friday Nights.** This club is patterned after a group of friends who would get together spontaneously on a Friday night with minimal notice and prep time.

3. **The Four Couples Club.** When my wife and I lived in Dover, Delaware, we had a club with a set group of four couples. The host couple would write the menu, delegate the recipes and then host the dinner party.

4. **Send Out the Email.** My daughter, Jennifer, gets credit for this one. She sends out an email a week in advance to a list for five or so couples. The email states the theme (e.g. Italian) and tells her friends she is making the entre (e.g. lasagna). She then asks who can come and what they would want to bring (e.g. side dish, dessert, beverages).

5. **"I Don't Cook, but I Know Where to Buy."** My daughter's mother-in-law, Helene, inspired this club. She doesn't cook, but she does a wonderful job of entertaining by bringing in take-out from local shops and restaurants.

In going through the different types of supper clubs, I will try to provide helpful examples of organization methods, menu ideas and, probably most important, people management. Supper clubs are a simple and fun way to bring people together to socialize over a meal.

Acknowledgements

There are lots of people who I need to thank for helping me with this book. First is my wife, Susan. She is the one who puts up with the "impromptu." Calling your wife at 3 pm to tell her that 10 people are coming to dinner at her house that night is dangerous with most wives. Susan has learned to go with the flow and does amazing job with it. She blames this book for being a hindrance to losing weight. All in all she has been the cornerstone behind making our supper clubs fun.

The original idea for the book comes from Lucien Vendome. My friend is an amazing chef and simply a very smart man. One night after a great meal and more than a little wine he said to me, "Lots of people write cookbooks. Did you ever think of writing a supper club book?" More than just providing the idea, Lucien taught me more about food and fine dining than anyone.

A special thanks has to go out to all the Supper Club friends we have had over the last 30-plus years. At the top of the list are the original Impromptu Friday Nights crew of the Floras, Chaudoins, Bells and Roses. They are the best. I also need to thank a few ladies that are the cornerstones of our neighborhood

Supper Club. Denise McMahon, Maureen O'Connor, Kathy Bell and Linda Stevens are the originators of the Classic Club that is so much a part of a lot of the book. There are also dozens more that have suffered through creations that didn't quite work and stories they have heard for the fifth time. Sorry, but I like telling stories about my cousins in Hawaii and summers in the Hamptons. It is amazing the obnoxious stuff people will put up with when the offset is a good meal.

I have to thank my children. They have suffered the most and have provided the most encouragement. This book is written for them and their generation. They keep telling me that they and their friends need it. My mom and sisters get special thanks. As the only boy growing up I was not allowed to cook, but I did get to learn. Mom and my sisters are good cooks, but more than that they are great hostesses. I also have to mention my daughter's in-laws. Helene and Rick Begun are the inspiration behind the "I Don't Cook, but I Know Where to Buy" chapter. It is one of my favorites. A special thanks goes out to my editor, Amanda Iles. More than editing she pushed me to add things that will hopefully make the book make more sense for millennials. She is just great. Finally, I want to thank the team at Morgan James Publishing. David Hancock and Aubrey Kosa have offered great support and encouragement.

My Background
With Supper Clubs and Food

My wife and I have been in supper clubs for over 30 years. We have been involved in clubs that were big, small, informal, formal and just about everything in between. And yes, we like to socialize over a good meal. We both grew up on the east coast, moved to California in the 1980s, and have lived in Memphis for over 20 years. One common denominator about everywhere we have lived is that our friends have enjoyed getting together over food and drinks.

I worked for Kraft Foods for 35 years. The bulk of my career was with Kraft Food Ingredients, the industrial business group that sold food ingredients to food manufacturers large and small. It uses culinary to demonstrate the benefits of its products to customers. Compared to "mother Kraft," KFI was a small company. Because of that, I was able take on many roles from Marketing, Sales, Finance and Operations. As the head of Marketing I was lucky to work with several great chefs and food scientists. In an earlier life, I ran the international business for KFI, which gave me the chance to travel the world and learn about different cuisines (I carry an extra 40 pounds to prove it).

A wise man once told me that there is nothing more boring than a 10-minute conversation about industrial food ingredients at a dinner party. The flip side to that is that there is nothing more fun than socializing over a great meal and a few drinks.

I come from a family of pretty good cooks. My parents loved to throw a dinner party. Actually, my father would decide he wanted to have a party and my mother would do all the work. She has been an adventurous foodie for over 70 years, and at 92 she is still an amazing hostess. My two sisters are also great cooks and hostesses. Growing up as the youngest male, I wasn't allowed to cook. When I married Susan in 1980, we started entertaining regularly. Susan would get the house ready and I would do the cooking. The earliest genesis of our supper clubs started with our friends the Waldmens while we lived in Dover, Delaware. Mark, Debbie, Susan and I would go out to dinner on a Friday night, and I would try to replicate the meal at home on Saturday night. From those early years to today, I truly enjoy the process of developing an event and spending time with friends and food.

Chapter 1

Finding the Right People

Getting people who mesh well together is always a challenge. One benefit of supper clubs is coming across all kinds of people. The good news is that you get to meet people. The bad news is that the chances of them being a great fit are pretty slim. One of the beauties of my supper club experience is that my wife and I have used the more formal supper club, where there are a lot of people, to find the smaller group that we really wanted to be friends with. In the end, dealing with a few jerks can be worth it if you get to know some very interesting people.

The solutions on how to find people to participate in a supper club are broad ranging:

- Neighborhood groups. This is one of the easiest ways to find people and conveniently located. The Classic Supper Club model is based on our neighborhood. We have a neighborhood association that publishes a newsletter. There is a section that advertises participation in the supper club. I have actually heard of people that bought a house in our neighborhood because they knew about the supper club.

- Internet groups. One site you could use to get started getting together with people over food is grubwithus.com. People get connected through the site, usually at a local restaurant.

- Colleagues. We all spend quite a bit of time with the people we work with. The subject of socializing over a meal is very easy to interject. When I lived in Delaware, I traveled with a guy I worked with. We would dine together on a Wednesday night, and the subject of my supper club would come up. It didn't take long for him to want to be part of the Saturday night supper club, where I would try to replicate the dishes we shared at a restaurant the previous Wednesday.

- Church groups.

- School groups.

- Facebook friends.

The supper clubs I have been involved with have led to real friendships. We have formed clubs from the wide array of sources listed above and have learned there is no one right way to find the right people. Trial and error is the only way. Going through a few bad experiences makes you appreciate the good ones.

Finding the right people has some real benefits. While most of us know a thing or two about wine, it is great to have a wine and beer experts in the group.

My friend Scott is the perfect example. He is excellent at paring the right wine with the menu. Scott, like many wine "experts," has an excellent wine collection and is great at offering up a few (or 10) delicious bottles from his cellar. Scott was such a good customer of the local wine store affectionately named "Germantown Baptist Wine and Liquor" by Scott's wife, Kathy, that when he moved, the wine store flew their flag at half-mast for weeks.

In my neighborhood, we are also blessed to have a "beer guy" as well. Tom Schoelkopf worked for Anheuser-Busch and is a great guy to have at a party. You can count on him to bring a good selection of Budweiser's classic product as well as some newer products they are developing. For many of our supper club events, people are asked to bring an appetizer. Tom is famous for asking, "Do you want me to cook, or should I just bring beer?" Somehow, the answers are pretty consistent.

It can be difficult to find the right people for a supper club. A good thing about being part of a larger group is that you get to meet a lot of people. Some you will like, and others, not so much.

One of my pet peeves is people using cell phones to make calls in the middle of a dinner party. I have to state up front that I, like many of us, am addicted to my cell phone. While I am not the nerdiest of nerds, in my circle of baby boomer friends, I am definitely up there as far as being technologically adept. If you really want to be bored, I can take you through the app I have developed to calculate golf bets. With this said, I also believe you have to draw the line.

There have been times where a guest has made a call from the table at a supper club dinner. One guy made multiple calls to his daughter while she was on a date. I guess he wanted us to know that his daughter was dating the starring baseball player from the local high school. (Ten years later, the pitcher has signed a $127 million dollar contract. He didn't marry the daughter.) For the next supper club, I wrote a menu and put a notice stating, "Please refrain from making cell phone calls from the dinner table" on it. I am not quite sure if it was because of the notice, but the offender dropped out of the club. Virtually the same scenario has happened more than once over the last 15 years.

With the above said, the rules on the use of cell phones at the dinner table are changing. My wife simply hates it. I find myself using it occasionally. Many millennials have phones as extended appendages. The key with a supper club is to establish ground rules that members can agree on or at least respect.

Set a Direction for the Club

Setting ground rules has been a topic of discussion in more than a few clubs I have been involved with. While there are all types of clubs from formal to very informal, it makes sense to have clear delineation of:

- Roles and responsibilities
- The degree of culinary complexity
- How often you meet
- Who pays for what
- The use of cell phones at the dinner table and other agreed-upon etiquette

Different types of clubs will require different levels of structure. There is no correct answer for all, and I have seen the level of structure change dramatically over time for different clubs. Like anything else, it has to do with people's personalities and preferences.

One of the key concepts behind a successful supper club is member participation. That means that the host has to give up complete control. My wife will tell you that I am a control freak when it comes to food. When giving up control, there is a certain level of danger and a risk to quality. We once had a dinner where I farmed out the salad. I thought it was a simple salad. What is simple for one can be a challenge for another. Our guest decided to mix the salad with the dressing hours before the dinner. By the time it came to serve it, the lettuce was a rancid looking off-color. Not wanting to risk the health of the other guests or hurt the feelings of the challenged salad maker, I tried to rescue the non-lettuce portions of the salad and whipped up a new salad with fresh lettuce and dressing.

The moral of this story is that it is best to try to correlate the complexity of the item being farmed out with the culinary skill level of the contributor. Beyond that, you have to be flexible.

Chapter 2:

Mise en Place

Preparation is a simple concept. If you can get things ready in advance, it takes the pressure off when you have to pull the meal together. The beauty of preparation is that it increases your chances of success and reduces stress. Having the work done in advance allows you to enjoy your guests and the event.

When it comes to food, the French really know their stuff. My work took me to France many times. With all the time I spent there, it is hard for me to remember a bad meal. I have had good meals in French airports. I even had a great meal in a factory cafeteria (I had these wax beans with shallots that were so good I spent years trying to replicate the flavor). One of the keys to French cuisine goes back to the culinary school lesson about mise en place.

Loosely translated, mise en place means "putting into place." My definition of mise en place includes all the key steps to get ready for a dinner: menu development, event planning and meal preparation. The goal is to get as much done in advance as possible.

I break the process down into four stages:

1. Theme creation
2. Menu development
3. Shopping list/work plan
4. Preparation

Theme Creation

Having a theme for the meal helps coordination. Quite often, the theme builds off of the main course. For me, an idea for a theme usually goes back to a restaurant, travel or media exposure. A great meal at an Italian restaurant can spark the theme. A meal I had in the Hamptons last summer could be the genesis. Increasingly, we can find themes in a TV show or an Internet article. Having a theme for your meal also creates a connection for your guests. As you are coming up with your theme, you want it to be something that will help your guests get excited about the meal.

Menu Development

The menu should build off of the theme. For menu ideas, I go back to the restaurants, travel and media sources where I found my idea for the theme. The Internet has become the primary research source for so many aspects of our lives, and menu development is certainly no exception.

I like to draft out the menu thinking about:

- Great meals I have had
- What is available in the local market (living in Memphis, it is what I saw at Costco last week)
- Local produce that is in season
- The skill level of the supper club members
- The culinary tools available (For example, I love homemade French fries. While making them in my home fry station is easy, it would be a little difficult to pull off in a kitchen without a deep fryer.)
- The time I have to prepare

Mise en place is all about organization with the goal of making the process easy. Again, the more you prepare, the less stressful it is at show time. I try to develop menus that require a minimal amount of last-minute preparation. This can be easier said than done. If it is a tradeoff between when I prepare a dish and quality, I will usually defer to quality.

I recently developed a menu for a supper club calling for mac and cheese. Working at Kraft, you might guess I had a little experience with pasta and cheese sauce. For years, we served M&C at trade show events and always struggled to keep the M&C saucy. The problem is that pasta acts like a sponge. If you make your M&C in advance, the chances are that it will be dry when you reheat it. I used to work with the guy that developed the cheese sauce for the original "Blue Box" product. It was always great to tell my kids' friends that I worked with the guy that invented Kraft Macaroni and Cheese. They would say, "Boy, he must be rich." To which I would respond, "No, he is just fat!" The solution to keeping your mac and cheese saucy is to increase the ratio of sauce to pasta and to have the sauce and pasta prepared in advance and mix the two at the last minute before reheating in the oven.

The Shopping List/Work Plan

The best way to get started on a shopping list is to use an existing menu or to outline one yourself. With the menu in hand, develop a list with all the ingredients you need. From that you can code the ingredients by store and by location in the market. I find that I like to buy different ingredients at different stores. For example, I think Costco meats* are great and I love the baguettes at the Fresh Market, so I will code my shopping list accordingly.

Following are two examples of a shopping list and work plan.

*At Kraft Food Ingredients, one of our customers was Costco. KFI had a really neat line called Flavors of Cooking. Our scientists had developed a flavor that could make a lesser cut of meat (e.g., chuck) taste like a more expensive cut (e.g., sirloin). In working with Costco, we explained this flavor to one of their chef/scientists. He responded, "Costco doesn't sell a lesser cuts of beef." As a consumer, I can confirm that what he said is true. By and large, Costco's meat quality is better than the standard supermarket fare.

Example 1

First, I take the menu (my California Cuisine Menu) and develop a shopping list and work plan:

- Menu item
- Ingredient
- Store to buy it in
- Where in the store to find it
- When to prepare it

Example 2

Second, I sort the shopping list by store and by section of the market.

Item/Ingredient	Store	Section
Shrimp/Avocado Quesadillas		
2 avocados	Kroger	Produce
2 limes	Kroger	Produce
½ lb. medium shrimp	Kroger	Meat/Seafood
1 small yellow onion	Kroger	Produce
1 red bell pepper	Kroger	Produce
5 ounces Monterey Jack Cheese	Kroger	Dairy
½ cup sour cream	Kroger	Dairy
1½ teaspoons chili powder	Kroger	Spices
4 flour tortillas	Kroger	Other
2 tablespoons vegetable oil	Kroger	Other
Salt and pepper to taste	Kroger	Other
Seared Beef Tenderloin		
2 pounds beef tenderloin	Fresh Market	Meat/Seafood
3½ tablespoons extra virgin olive oil	Costco	Other
1 small bunch spring greens	Fresh Market	Produce
4 tablespoons capers	Costco	Other
½ cup shaved Parmesan	Costco	Dairy
1 tablespoon lime juice	Kroger	Produce
1 pack Baja rub	Kroger	Other
Mustard Horseradish Sauce		
⅔ cup sour cream	Kroger	Dairy
¼ cup Dijon mustard	Kroger	Other
2 tablespoons olive oil	Costco	Other

Item/Ingredient	Store	Section
2 tablespoons prepared horseradish sauce	Kroger	Dairy
2 tablespoons chopped fresh tarragon	Fresh Market	Produce
Dressing		
2 shallots	Kroger	Produce
2 whole star anise	Kroger	Other
⅔ cup vegetable oil	Kroger	Other
6 tablespoons fresh orange juice	Kroger	Other
1 teaspoon port	Wine/Liquor	Other
Endive, Pear and Blue Cheese Salad		
4 firm Bosc pears	Kroger	Produce
8 heads Belgian endive	Kroger	Produce
10 ounces Stilton cheese	Kroger	Dairy
½ cup walnut halves	Costco	Other
Fresh parsley	Fresh Market	Produce
Sesame Chilean Sea Bass		
8 sea bass fillets (4–5 ounces each)	Fresh Market	Seafood
4 tablespoons white sesame seeds	Kroger	Other
4 tablespoons black sesame seeds	Kroger	Other
½ cup Japanese breadcrumbs	Kroger	Other
2½ sticks of salted butter	Kroger	Dairy
1 bunch green asparagus	Kroger	Produce
2 cups black rice	Fresh Market	Other
½ cup red bell pepper	Kroger	Produce
½ cup fresh chives	Fresh Market	Produce
1 package McCormick white sauce	Kroger	Other
½ cup diced shallots	Kroger	Produce
1 tablespoon wasabi paste	Fresh Market	Other
2 tablespoons soy sauce	Kroger	Other
Kosher salt	Kroger	Other
Freshly ground pepper	Kroger	Other
Poached Peaches		
4 hard peaches	Kroger	Produce
1 cup white wine	Kroger	Other
3½ cups cold water		

Item/Ingredient	Store	Section
1½ cups sugar	Kroger	Other
1 whole vanilla bean (or 2 teaspoons vanilla extract)	Kroger	Other
1 13-ounce jar Bonne Maman Wild Blueberry Preserves		
1 lime		
Ice Cream		
Häagen-Dazs Vanilla Ice Cream	Kroger	Frozen
Blueberry Compote	Kroger	Other
1 13-ounce jar Bonne Maman Wild Blueberry Preserves		
Example 2: Shopping List Ingredient		
5 ounces Monterey Jack cheese	Kroger	Dairy
½ cup sour cream	Kroger	Dairy
⅔ cup sour cream	Kroger	Dairy
2 tablespoons prepared horseradish sauce	Kroger	Dairy
10 ounces Stilton cheese	Kroger	Dairy
2½ sticks of salted butter	Kroger	Dairy
1½ sticks butter	Kroger	Dairy
1 Häagen-Dazs vanilla ice cream	Kroger	Frozen
½ pound medium shrimp	Kroger	Meat/Seafood
4 flour tortillas	Kroger	Other
2 tablespoons vegetable oil	Kroger	Other
Salt and pepper to taste	Kroger	Other
1 pack Baja rub	Kroger	Other
¼ cup Dijon mustard	Kroger	Other
2 whole star anise	Kroger	Other
⅔ cup vegetable oil	Kroger	Other
6 tablespoons fresh orange juice	Kroger	Other
4 tablespoons white sesame seeds	Kroger	Other
4 tablespoons black sesame seeds	Kroger	Other
½ cup Japanese breadcrumbs	Kroger	Other
1 package McCormick white sauce	Kroger	Other
2 tablespoons soy sauce	Kroger	Other
Kosher salt	Kroger	Other
Freshly ground pepper	Kroger	Other
1 cup sugar	Kroger	Other

Item/Ingredient	Store	Section
4 squares Baker's unsweetened chocolate	Kroger	Other
3 eggs	Kroger	Other
1 tablespoon vanilla	Kroger	Other
1 cup flour	Kroger	Other
1 cup sugar	Kroger	Other
2 avocados	Kroger	Produce
2 lines	Kroger	Produce
1 small yellow onion	Kroger	Produce
1 red bell pepper	Kroger	Produce
1 tablespoon lime juice	Kroger	Produce
2 shallots	Kroger	Produce
4 firm Bosc pears	Kroger	Produce
8 heads Belgian endive	Kroger	Produce
1 bunch green asparagus	Kroger	Produce
½ cup red bell pepper	Kroger	Produce
½ cup diced shallots	Kroger	Produce
1½ cups blueberries	Kroger	Produce
1½ cups raspberries	Kroger	Produce
1½ teaspoon chili powder	Kroger	Spice
½ cup shaved Parmesan	Costco	Dairy
3½ tablespoons extra virgin olive oil	Costco	Other
4 tablespoons capers	Costco	Other
2 tablespoons olive oil	Costco	Other
½ cup walnut halves	Costco	Other
1 cup chopped walnuts	Costco	Other
2 pounds beef tenderloin	Fresh Market	Meat/Seafood
8 sea bass fillets (4–5 ounces each)	Fresh Market	Meat/Seafood
2 cups black rice	Fresh Market	Other
1 tablespoon wasabi paste	Fresh Market	Produce
2 tablespoons chopped fresh tarragon	Fresh Market	Produce
Fresh parsley	Fresh Market	Produce
½ cup fresh chives	Fresh Market	Produce
1 ounce Grand Marnier	Wine/Liquor	Other
1 teaspoon port	Wine/Liquor	Other

Preparation

Here is where the real work has to be done. I try to follow the work plan, but things always come up. Your goal should be to get as much of your prep work done as early as possible. The one thing they never show you on cooking shows is all the prep work that goes into a meal. Great chefs spend an inordinate amount of their time slicing and dicing. The best chef I know, who has as much staff as anyone, is getting close to retirement and told me, "I am tired of spending my life slicing and dicing."

While it is the nature of the beast, the beauty of working with good chefs is watching their tricks of the trade that expedite the process. Simple things can save a lot of time. I was once working on an event in a Chicago hotel and a sous-chef was preparing green beans. I always cut the ends off one bean at a time. The experienced chef takes 10 beans at a time, taps the ends on a table to line them up and then trims ten at a time. Simple!

I believe in food processors, mandolines and good knives. Some people have complained that my menus are too time consuming. When talking to one complainant, she told me she spent half an hour chopping onions. I responded by asking her if she owned a food processor. While she did own one, she would never have thought of using it for chopping onions. Try it; they work great. There are some things that need a more precise dice, but for the bulk of your chopping needs, a food processor suffices. Whenever you can find a shortcut, go for it.

Hosting a successful dinner requires preparation. If you have everything "put into place" (mise en place), you reduce the stress of entertaining.

Menu Example

The idea for this menu I developed a few years back came from a trip to the west coast. To say it is eclectic is probably an understatement, but that is pretty much my interpretation of California cuisine—anything.

Time and Temperature Caveat

Throughout the book time and temperature data is provided. I have always struggled with the question, How long do I cook this for? The answer is that it depends. A great example happened a few weeks ago. My daughter was cooking my Char-Roasted Ham for her in-laws. She called me panicked about two hours into the process saying it has been cooking on the grill for two hours and isn't done yet. A few questions later I learned that she, her husband and her father in law had been checking the ham every 15 minutes by lifting the grill lid. Lift the lid and lose the heat, and it could take a month to cook.

Time and temperature can be influenced by many factors:

- Oven/stovetop/grill temperatures vary.
- Opening oven/grills.
- One man's high is another man's medium.
- Moving the meat on the grill is bad. Constant flipping is worse.

The time and temperatures provided are based on research and experience. Ranges provide a safety net. Just make sure you enjoy the learning.

California Cuisine Menu
Appetizer
Shrimp and Avocado Quesadillas
First Course
Seared Baja Beef Tenderloin with Spring Greens, Parmesan and Mustard/ Horseradish Sauce
Second Course
Endive, Pear and Blue Cheese Salad
Main Course
Sesame Chilean Sea Bass with Wasabi/Soy Beurre Blanc Sauce, Asparagus and Black Rice
Dessert
Poached Peaches with Vanilla Ice Cream and Blueberry Compote

shrimp and avocado quesadilla with southwestern sauce

Ingredients

1 large shallot, peeled and cut into ¼-inch slices

½ cup olive oil

½ pound medium shrimp, raw, deveined and shell removed

12 10-inch flour tortillas

8 ounces Monterey Jack cheese, shredded

1 ripe avocado, peeled, pitted and cut into ⅜-inch slices

Salt and pepper to taste

1 teaspoon ancho chili powder

½ cup chopped fresh cilantro

Southwestern Sauce (see page 32)

Cookware Needed

10 or 12 inch sauté (or frying) pan

Baking sheet

Serves 8 people

1. In a medium sauté pan, sauté shallots in olive oil until translucent (7 minutes).

2. In the same pan, lightly sauté shrimp in olive oil until they just start to turn pink. Be careful not to overcook as you will cook them a second time when frying the quesadilla.

3. Lay out 6 tortillas.

4. Sprinkle on a layer of cheese.

5. Add shallots.

6. Add shrimp.

7. Add avocado.

8. Sprinkle with salt, pepper and chili powder.

9. Add the top tortilla.

10. On a hot skillet or grill top, add a thin layer of oil, then grill each quesadilla. Each side should be grilled for 3–5 minutes or until the tortilla becomes golden brown.

11. Cook the quesadillas in batches and transfer to a cookie sheet.

12. 20 minutes before serving, reheat the quesadillas on the cookie sheet in a 350°F oven.

13. Slice quesadillas into wedges.

14. Using a squirt bottle, add zig-zag lines of the Southwestern Sauce.

15. Sprinkle with cilantro and serve.

Cook Time	Temperature
Sauté shallot	Medium-high for 5-7 min
Sauté shrimp	Medium-high for 3-4 min
Cook quesadilla (per side)	Medium-high for 3-5 min
Reheat quesadilla	350°F for 15-20 min
Total	**26–36 min**

Step	Prep Time
Peel/dice shallot	4–6 min
Remove shell/devein shrimp	5–10 min
Shred cheese	3–5 min
Final assembly and presentation	5–10 min
Total	**17–31 min**

seared baja beef tenderloin with spring greens and parmesan, mustard and horseradish sauce

Ingredients

6 ounces beef filet mignon, cut into medallions 1½ inches around and ⅜ inch thick

½ cup Baja rub, made by whisking together:

2 tablespoons cornstarch

1 tablespoon sweet paprika

1 teaspoon chili powder

1 teaspoon garlic powder

1 teaspoon onion powder

1 teaspoon kosher salt

¼ cup olive oil

3 cups mixed spring greens

Parmesan, Mustard and Horseradish Sauce

Cookware Needed

10 or 12 inch sauté (or frying) pan

Medium-sized mixing bowl

Serves 8 people

1. Dredge beef medallions in Baja rub.

2. Preheat a sauté pan with a thin layer of olive oil until oil smokes.

3. Quickly sauté the beef medallions a few minutes on each side until cooked to medium rare.

4. Plate on a bed of spring greens.

5. Top with Parmesan, Mustard and Horseradish Sauce (see below).

Step	Prep Time
Whick Baja Rub together	3-5 min
Prep beef	5–10 min
Final assembly and presentation	5–10 min
Total	**13–25 min**

Cook Time	Temperature
Sear beef	High for 2-3 min per side
Total	4–6 min

parmesan, mustard and horseradish sauce

Ingredients

¼ **cup mayonnaise**

¼ **cup sour cream**

2 tablespoons finely grated Parmesan cheese

2 tablespoons Dijon mustard

2 tablespoons prepared horseradish

1 teaspoon honey

In a medium bowl, whisk the ingredients together.

endive, pear and blue cheese salad

Ingredients

4 heads endive

2 15-ounce cans pear halves

½ cup Vinaigrette (see below)

4 ounces blue cheese, crumbled

8 strips bacon, diced into 1-inch pieces and sautéed until crispy

1. Lay out 8 plates.

2. Add 4 large endive leaves to each plate.

3. Place a pear half in the middle.

4. Drizzle with Vinaigrette.

5. Add blue cheese.

6. Sprinkle on bacon.

vinaigrette

Ingredients

2 cloves garlic

1 teaspoon kosher salt

3 tablespoons white wine vinegar

2 teaspoons Dijon mustard

1 teaspoon honey

½ cup olive oil

1 tablespoon chopped fresh dill

Cookware Needed

10 or 12 inch sauté (or frying) pan

Medium-sized mixing bowl

Serves 8 people

1. Chop/mash garlic in the kosher salt.

2. In a small bowl, whisk together garlic, salt, white wine vinegar, Dijon mustard and honey.

3. Drizzle in olive oil slowly while whisking vigorously. Whisk until well emulsified.

4. Add dill and whisk until incorporated

Step	Prep Time
Whick Baja Rub together	3-5 min
Prep beef	5–10 min
Final assembly and presentation	5–10 min
Total	**13–25 min**

Cook Time	Temperature
Sauté bacon	Medium for 5-8 min per side
Total	**10–16 min**

Step	Prep Time
Final assembly and presentation	5–10 min
Total	**5-10 min**

sesame chilean sea bass

Ingredients

8 4-ounce pieces Chilean sea bass

Salt and pepper

½ cup olive oil

4 tablespoons white sesame seeds

4 tablespoons black sesame seeds

4 tablespoons butter

Wasabi Beurre Blanc Sauce (see below)

Cookware Needed

Two 10 or 12 inch sauté (or frying) pan

Serves 8 people

1. Preheat oven to 400°F.

2. Pat the sea bass fillets dry* and sprinkle with salt and pepper.

3. Brush with olive oil.

4. Dredge in mixture of white and black sesame seeds.

5. In two sauté pans, heat 2 tablespoons butter and 4 tablespoons olive oil in each until just smoking.

6. Sauté 4 filets in each pan (so that they are well spaced) until the first side is golden brown.

7. Flip to the second side and place in oven.

8. Cook for about 10 minutes or until nicely crisped on the outside and about 83% cooked through. (Note: Make sure to not overcook the sea bass.)

* Have you ever wondered how top end restaurants get a good crust on seafood when they pan roast? The key is to get the fish really dry before searing. A trick that good chefs will use is to dry the fish by wrapping it in a paper towel and placing it in the refrigerator for an hour or two.

Cook Time	Temperature
Sear see bass (per side on stovetop)	Medium-high for 3-5 min
Finish in oven	400°F for 8-10 min
Total	**14–20 min**

Step	Prep Time
Prep sea bass	5–10 min
Prep beef	5-10 min
Final assembly and presentation	5–10 min
Total	**15-30 min**

poached peaches with vanilla ice cream and blueberry compote

Ingredients

4 hard peaches

1 cup white wine

3½ cups cold water

1½ cups sugar

1 whole vanilla bean (or 2 teaspoons vanilla extract)

2 tablespoons cornstarch

1 pint Häagen-Dazs vanilla ice cream

1 13-ounce jar Bonne Maman Wild Blueberry Preserves

1 lime

Cookware Needed

Large saucepan

Whisk

Serves 8 people

1. Cut peaches in half and remove pits.

2. In a large saucepan, combine wine, 2 cups water, sugar, and seeds scraped from the vanilla bean.

3. Bring to a simmer over medium heat, whisking to dissolve sugar.

4. Add the peaches and poach for 15 minutes or until peaches are fork-tender.

5. Remove peaches and set aside to cool.

6. Bring wine/water/sugar mix to a boil.

7. Dissolve the cornstarch in 1½ cups cold water and add it to the boiling mixture to thicken.

8. Set aside to cool.

9. Zest the lime. Reserve the fruit for another use.

Plating

1. Place a peach half in a shallow dessert bowl.

2. Add 3–4 tablespoons of wine/water/sugar mix to the bottom of the bowl.

3. Place a scoop of vanilla ice cream on the peach.

4. Add a large dollop of blueberry preserves on top of the ice cream.

5. Sprinkle the plate with lime zest.

Cook Time	Temperature
Poach peaches	Medium-high for 13-17 min
Thicken poaching liquid into a syrup	Medium-high for 5-10 min
Total	**18–27 min**

Step	Prep Time
Cut peaches and remove pits	3-5 min
Prep poaching liquid	2-3 min
Cool	10-20 min
Assemble	5–10 min
Total	**20–38 min**

southwestern sauce

Ingredients
¼ cup mayonnaise
¼ cup sour cream
¼ cup Kraft Original BBQ sauce
1 teaspoon ancho chili powder
2 tablespoons fresh lime juice

Cookware Needed
Medium-sized mixing bowl
Squirt bottle

1. In a small bowl, whisk together all ingredients until well blended.

2. Transfer to a squirt bottle.

wasabi beurre blanc sauce

Ingredients
4 tablespoons unsalted butter
3 tablespoons finely minced shallot
¼ cup white wine
1 cup chicken stock
2 teaspoons cornstarch
¼ cup cold water
1 tablespoon wasabi powder
¼ cup heavy cream

Cookware Needed
Two 10 or 12 inch sauté
(or frying) pans

1. In a medium sauté pan, melt butter.

2. Add shallot and sauté at a low temperature until translucent.

3. Deglaze pan with white wine.

4. Add chicken stock and cook until reduced by a third.

5. Mix the cornstarch in a small bowl with cold water.

6. Add the cornstarch mixture to stock to thicken.

7. Whisk in wasabi powder.

8. Add cream, whisk and serve.

asparagus

Ingredients

1 pound asparagus with ends trimmed

¼ cup olive oil

Salt and pepper

Cookware Needed

Baking sheet

1. Brush asparagus with olive oil.

2. Sprinkle with salt and pepper.

3. Place in one layer on a cookie sheet.

4. Cook in a 380°F oven for 15–20 minutes until crisped.

Step	Prep Time
Prep asparagus	4–6 min
Total	4-6 min

Cook Time	Temperature
Roast asparagus	380°F for15–20 min
Total	15-20 min

black rice

Ingredients

2 cups black rice

Cook following the instructions on the package.

Plating

1. Place sea bass in the middle of the plate.

2. Add asparagus.

3. Add black rice.

4. Sauce the plate liberally with the Wasabi Beurre Blanc Sauce.

Prep Schedule—Mise en Place (for a Saturday evening dinner)

Thursday
Make Southwestern Sauce*
Make horseradish sauce*
Friday
Poach peaches
Saturday
10:00AM Sauté bacon
11:00   Prep sea bass
12:00PM Prep and cook quesadillas
1:00   Prep asparagus
2:00   Make black rice
4:00   Place asparagus in oven
5:00   Make beurre blanc sauce
6:00   Set out sauces
6:10   Place quesadillas in oven
6:20   Sauté/roast sea bass
6:30   Assemble and lay out quesadillas
6:35   Guests arrive, serve wine
6:45   Chit chat
7:00   Assemble and serve salad
7:10   Sear beef
7:15   Assemble and serve beef
7:30   Assemble and serve sea bass garlic bread
7:40   Assemble and serve dessert.

> * Sauces can be made up to a week in advance.

Wine Recommendations

Wine	Origin	Composition	Price
Red			
Apothic Blend	Modesto, CA	Red Blend	$12.00
14 Hands Cabernet	Columbia Valley, WA	Cabernet Sauvignon	$10.99
Prisoner	Napa, CA	Red Blend	$35.00
White			
Cambria Chardonnay	Santa Maria, CA	Chardonnay	$20.00
Robert Mondavi Chardonnay	Napa Valley, CA	Chardonnay	$17.99
Atemms Pinot Grigio Ramato	Venezia Giulia, Italia	Pinot Grigio	$12.25

Chapter 3

The Classic Club

The Classic Club is the most formal of the different types of supper clubs. This section is patterned after a club my wife and I have been part of in our current neighborhood for over 20 years and with a club we had back in Dover, Delaware, during the 1980s. This club has the most structure, with quite a bit of definition around roles, responsibilities and frequency.

The Club Makeup

There are 20 "regular couples" and 30 "substitute couples." For each dinner, four couples get together at the host's house for dinner. The substitute list is a great way for newcomers to learn about the club without the full responsibility of hosting, which can be a little daunting. Correspondingly, quite a few members stay on the substitute list for years.

The Board

There is a four-member board that sets the structure. Our neighborhood association sponsors our supper club. Two people have been at the core of the board since its inception in the early 1990s and have been the force behind providing the structure. The role of the board involves:

- Writing the menus or assigning someone to write the menus
- Setting the outline of the dates
- Organizing annual kickoff and closing events
- Facilitating scheduling solutions (e.g., whenever there is a last-minute dropout or need for last-minute substitutes)

Dates

Our club has found that six dates work well:

- Kickoff event (early September)
- September dinner
- October dinner
- February dinner
- March dinner
- Year-end event (April/May)

The summer just doesn't work with vacations, travel and kids being out of school.

Host Responsibilities

- The hosts will be given the menu approximately two weeks in advance. The two weeks' notice rule gives the hosts time to plan or bail if they find the menu too challenging.
- The hosts will then distribute the menu to their guests, designating who is responsible for which items.
- With the distribution, they set the date, time and place for the dinner. They can also move the date within a window of a few weeks to best accommodate the schedules of the other couples.

- If they have an opening with an early dropout, the hosts are encouraged to invite neighbors or friends to the club as a way to promote the club to new participants.
- The hosts are responsible for making the main dish (or two) and assigning the other guests to make the remaining dishes.
- The hosts provide the before and after dinner drinks as well as any table decorations.

Costs

Costs for making the dishes are tracked by each couple. At the end of the evening, all costs for food and wine will be totaled then divided equally among the four couples, with each couple paying one-fourth of the total meal cost.

Cost Example

	Costs	Avg. Cost	Net
Couple 1 (hosts)	$175.00	−$67.00	$108.00
Couple 2	35.00	−67.00	−32.00
Couple 3	15.00	−67.00	−52.00
Couple 4	43.00	−67.00	−24.00
	$268.00	−$268.00	$0.00

Average cost $67.00

It is amazing how costs are virtually never an issue. With a little planning and discretion, supper clubs are economical even for the more cost-conscious. You can have a good meal and social event for less than $70 per couple. The cost driver is usually the alcohol. The rule we have followed is to target "reasonably" priced wines. Although participants have defined "reasonable" differently, on average we have probably been in the $20-a-bottle range, though there have been notable exceptions for costs and quantities. I can tell you that our young kids did once question the number of wine bottles in the recycling bin after one particularly fun event.

With new people coming in and out of the club, there have been a few surprises. One new club member built in the cost of a pot she bought for the event into her total contribution. I can't say that couple is still part of the club. The rule we have lived by is that if we incur a cost because we want to try something different or more expensive than the norm, we simply absorb that cost. With this said, some hosts are more popular than others.

Substitutes

It is the responsibility of each couple to call a substitute member if they cannot make the supper. It is also the responsibility of each couple to let the host couple know as soon as possible if they can't attend. Managing dates and getting substitutes can be one of the more daunting aspects of such a large club. Over the years, the standard operating procedures have changed quite a bit. I have found that if you can be a little flexible on dates and communicate with people, getting subs is pretty easy. At the discretion of the hosts, occasionally, two groups have merged. Personally, I am a fan of the "more the merrier." Most menus are easily scalable with some pretty basic math skills. My wife, on the practical side, gets nervous about numbers.

While it is initially the responsibility of each couple to get a sub, that chore shifts to the hosts pretty regularly. The hosts really get to dictate, so the fill-ins can be friends, family members, neighbors or whomever. There have been situations over the years where people have moved from the neighborhood and still wanted to be part of the club. In the end, the "more the merrier" rule has won out.

The hosts can also decide to move the supper up or back a week or two at their discretion or based on the availability of the guests. Moving it up becomes a bit more of a challenge as this author quite often puts off menu distribution.

Rotation

The following is a schedule that minimizes having "repeats" on the guest list. The basic structure of the club has twenty "regular" members, and there are four dinner parties (September, October, February and March). The challenge is to minimize the repeats (getting scheduled with the same couple more than once.

The following formula works pretty well.

September	Party 1	Party 2	Party 3	Party 4	Party 5
Couple 1 (hosts)	11	15	13	16	19
Couple 2	3	2	8	10	17
Couple 3	5	12	1	14	18
Couple 4	6	7	20	9	4
October	Party 1	Party 2	Party 3	Party 4	Party 5
Couple 1 (hosts)	3	2	8	10	17
Couple 2	12	1	14	18	5
Couple 3	20	9	4	6	7
Couple 4	19	11	15	13	16
February	Party 1	Party 2	Party 3	Party 4	Party 5
Couple 1 (hosts)	5	12	1	14	18
Couple 2	4	6	7	20	9
Couple 3	13	16	19	11	15
Couple 4	2	8	10	17	3
March	Party 1	Party 2	Party 3	Party 4	Party 5
Couple 1 (hosts)	6	7	20	9	4
Couple 2	19	11	15	13	16
Couple 3	2	8	10	17	3
Couple 4	14	18	5	12	1

Members

Number	Name
1	Smith
2	Johnson
3	Williams
4	Jones
5	Brown
6	Davis
7	Miller
8	Wilson
9	Moore
10	Taylor
11	Anderson
12	Thomas
13	Jackson
14	White
15	Harris
16	Martin
17	Thompson
18	Garcia
19	Martinez
20	Robinson

The way it works is that at the kickoff event, everyone is given the schedule. Each couple is given a number. The first thing you do is circle your number to find out when you host and who you are paired with at each supper.

So in our rotation example, at the September party member 11 (Anderson) are the hosts and will have members 3 (Williams), 5 (Brown), and 6 (Davis) as their guests.

Repeats can be a challenge, and so can neighborhood feuds. Over time, there tend to be situations where it is just safer to not have certain couples at the same dinner table. This scheduling challenge can fall back to the board but can be more civilly handled with the "we can't make it that weekend" excuse.

The Kickoff Event

It is great to get all the participants together at the start of the year to discuss the calendar and how the club works, although finding a volunteer to host the event can be a challenge. The format that has worked well is to set the time and place and ask everyone to bring an appetizer to share and a beverage of choice. We charge nominal dues of $5 per year to cover miscellaneous expenses and gain commitment.

The Year-End Event

If it is hard to get someone to host the kickoff event, it is even more difficult to get a volunteer for the year-end soiree. A common fallback is to have a get together at a local restaurant. The year-end event is basically socialization. It also presents a good opportunity to reprise the year over a few adult beverages. Some good ideas have come from this event and have been incorporated into the next year's supper club.

Menu Example

I love tasting menus. What is more fun than getting to taste a variety of different items? Two challenges of preparing a tasting menu are:

1. Keeping the prep/coordination simple
2. Managing portions

With the above said, for some of us, half the fun is in the prep and the challenge of coordinating a large menu. As far as portion size, I like to warn participants that the meal will be a marathon, not a sprint, and I make sure they know I will not be offended if everyone doesn't eat everything.

Tasting Menu

First Course

Romaine wedge with blue cheese vinaigrette, bacon, heirloom tomatoes, and homemade croutons

Gorgonzola Stuffed Shrimp wrapped in Bacon

Second Course

Pan roasted cod loin served with Sauce Americane, rice and green beans

Third Course

Rack of lamb Provençal served with a béarnaise blush sauce, pommes frites and sautéed asparagus

Dessert

Carrot Cake and German Chocolate Cake Mini Parfait

romaine wedge with gorgonzola vinaigrette and croutons

vinaigrette

Ingredients

3 cloves garlic, finely diced with 2 teaspoons kosher salt

2 heaping tablespoons Dijon mustard

2 tablespoons white wine vinegar

Juice of 1 lemon

2 teaspoons honey

1 cup extra virgin olive oil

2 tablespoons Italian parsley, finely chopped

1½ cups roughly grated Gorgonzola cheese (buy a block at Costco—better quality at half the price)

Cookware Needed

Nixing bowl

Wire whisk

Serves 8 people as Tasting Menu

1. In a large mixing bowl, add garlic, mustard, vinegar, lemon juice, and honey. Whisk together.

2. Drizzle in the olive oil, whisking vigorously. Keep whisking until the vinaigrette is nicely emulsified.

3. Whisk in the Italian parsley and Gorgonzola.

4. Set aside or refrigerate.

Step	Prep Time
Dice/mash garlic	3-5 min
Chop parsley	2-3 min
Grate Gorgonzola	3-4 min
Whisk	3-5 min
Total	**11-17 min**

croutons

Ingredients

7 cloves garlic

¼–½ cup olive oil

½ French baguette,
cut into 1 × 1 inch pieces

Cookware Needed

10 or 12 inch sauté
(or frying) pans

Serves 8 people as Tasting Menu

Step	Prep Time
Chop garlic	2-3 min
Cut up baguette	3-4 min
Total	**5-7 min**

1. Preheat oven to 380°F.

2. Finely chop garlic.

3. In a large sauté pan, sauté garlic in ¼ cup olive oil for 4 minutes over medium-low heat until garlic softens.

4. Add baguette pieces and stir so that they are coated in olive oil (add a little more oil if necessary) under high heat.

5. When the bread starts to brown, shift the sauté pan into the oven.

6. Bake for 5–10 minutes or until the croutons are crunchy brown.

Final Prep/Plating

1. Place romaine quarters onto a full-size plate.

2. Drizzle liberally with Gorgonzola Vinaigrette.

3. Add tomato/olive mixture.

4. Add croutons and bacon.

5. Top with red onion rings.

6. Serve.

Cook Time	Temperature
Sauté garlic	Medium-low for 4-5 min
Sauté bread/garlic/oil	Medium-high for 5-6 min
Bake croutons	380° for 5-10 min
Total	**14–21 min**

romaine wedge

Ingredients

2 romaine hearts
(¼ heart per person)

½ pound bacon,
cut into 1-inch pieces

1 small package (1 pint) grape
tomatoes, cut into halves

24 pitted Kalamata olives

3 green onions, roughly
chopped into ¼-inch pieces

2 cloves garlic, cut into paper-
thin slices

3 tablespoons olive oil

Kosher salt and freshly ground
pepper

16 rings red onion, thinly sliced
and separated

Cookware Needed

Mixing bowl

Wire whisk

10 or 12 inch sauté (or frying)
pans

Serves 8 people as Tasting
Menu

1. Trim romaine hearts to 8 inches in length. Cut into quarters lengthwise. Cover with a damp paper towel and set aside.

2. Brown the bacon and set aside. (Don't pick.)

3. In a mixing bowl, combine the tomatoes, olives, green onion, garlic and olive oil.

4. Add salt and pepper to taste.

5. Mix and set aside.

6. Set aside red onion for topping.

Step	Prep Time
Trim and quarter romaine	3-5 min
Dice bacon	2-3 min
Make tomato/ olive mixture	2-3 min
Final assembly and presentation	5-10 min
Total	**12-21 min**

Cook Time	Temperature
Sauté bacon	Medium for 7-10 min
Total	**7-10 min**

gorgonzola-stuffed shrimp wrapped in bacon

Ingredients

10 strips Oscar Mayer* bacon

16 jumbo shrimp
(8–12 per pound count)

5 ounces Gorgonzola cheese

Kosher salt and pepper

Cookware Needed

Baking pan

Grill

Oven/broiler

Grill/grid

Serves 8 people
as Tasting Menu

* Yes I worked for Kraft for 35 years and still own stock in the company. Past that noise, I like to use Oscar Mayer bacon in this dish because of the mild smoke flavor. Quite often, the smoke flavor in bacon is too strong and simply overpowers the shrimp.

1. Preheat oven to 400°F.

2. With a large kitchen knife, slice the bacon lengthwise and place the half strips on a baking sheet to precook them in the oven. This should only take about 5 minutes as you want to slightly render the bacon but not cook it to a point where it isn't still pliable.

3. Take most of the shell off of the shrimp, leaving the tail/shell on, and devein the shrimp.

4. With a sharp knife, butterfly-cut the shrimp in half, being careful to split it but not cut through.

5. Lay the butterflied shrimp on a work surface. Sprinkle with salt and pepper and place a stick of Gorgonzola (1½ inches long and ⅜ inch thick) on each shrimp.

6. Wrap the shrimp and Gorgonzola in the bacon strip. There is no simple way to do this. You just have to wrestle with the bacon and shrimp, trying to get good coverage and as tight a wrap as possible.

7. Place the bacon-wrapped shrimp on a grill grid or grate.

8. Preheat grill to 500–600°F (as hot as you can get it).

9. Preheat your oven to broil.

10. Cook your shrimp on the grill until the bottom of the shrimp is nicely charred.

11. Finish the shrimp under the broiler in your oven to crisp the bacon.

Cook Time	Temperature
Precook bacon	400°F for 3-5 min
Grill shrimp	500–600°F for 5-10 min
Finish Shrimp under broiler	High for 3-5 min
Total	**11–20 min**

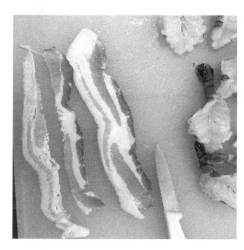

Step	Prep Time
Prep bacon	3-5 min
Prep shrimp	5-10 min
Cool	10-20 min
Assemble	5–10 min
Total	**23–45 min**

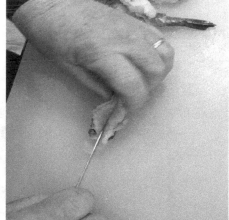

pan-roasted cod loin

Ingredients

1 cod loin (about 5 ounces)

2 tablespoons unsalted butter

2 tablespoons olive oil

Salt and pepper to taste

Cookware Needed

10 or 12 inch sauté (or frying) pan

Serves 8 people as Tasting Menu

1. Preheat oven to 400°F.

2. Clean the cod loin under running water and pat dry. To get a good sear on the cod, it has to be really dry. The best way to do this is to wrap it in a paper towel and place in the refrigerator for 5 hours.

3. Melt the butter and olive oil in a sauté pan and heat until it just begins to simmer under a medium-high heat.

4. Sauté the cod for 4–5 minutes on each side, getting a good sear and a golden brown color.

5. Place the pan into a 400°F oven for another 10 minutes until the loin is just cooked through. Do not overcook.

Step	Prep Time
Prep cod	3-5 min
Final assembly and presentation	5–10 min
Total	**20–38 min**

Cook Time	Temperature
Sauté cod (per side)	High for 5-6 min
Finish in oven	400°F for 8-10 min
Total	**18–22 min**

sauce americaine

This is one of my all-time favorite sauces. Think about it: lobster, butter, cream and brandy…how can it not taste fantastic? I have friends that I offered a taste of this off the stove and the next thing I knew, they were sitting at the pot on the stove with spoons, drinking the sauce as if it were the nectar of the gods. The beauty of this sauce is that while it is technically a lobster sauce, it can be made without lobster. I have made it by substituting shrimp stock and even clam juice for the lobster stock. Somehow, the fish note with cream and a little red coloring from the tomato paste make this sauce work.

lobster stock

Ingredients
½ **cup onion, diced**
½ **cup carrots, diced**
½ **cup celery, diced**
3 tablespoons olive oil
4 cups water
1 lobster

Cookware Needed
Large pot
10 or 12 inch sauté (or frying) pan

Serves 8 People as Tasting Menu

1. In a good-sized pot, sauté the onion, carrots and celery in olive oil until translucent.

2. Add the water and bring to a boil.

3. Add the lobster and cook for five to ten minutes.

4. Take the lobster out and set aside.

5. Strain the remaining solids out of the broth and set aside.

Step	Prep Time
Prep lobster stock	5-10 min
Final assembly and presentation	5-10 min
Total	**10-20 min**

sauce

Ingredients

1 tablespoon olive oil

½ cup shallots, sliced

2 tablespoons garlic, sliced

1½ tablespoons black peppercorns

½ cup brandy

2 cups lobster stock

2 tablespoons tomato paste

¼ cup whipping cream

1 basil sprig

2 tarragon sprigs

½ teaspoon fine sea salt

⅛ teaspoon freshly ground white pepper

½ cup unsalted butter, cut into large pieces

1 heaping teaspoon of cornstarch dissolved in cold water

1. In a large sauté pan, heat the olive oil. Sauté shallots, garlic and peppercorns over a medium-low heat until the shallots and garlic are translucent.

2. Deglaze the pan with the brandy.

3. Add the lobster stock, bring to a boil and reduce by one-third.

4. Whisk in the tomato paste.

5. Add the cream, basil, tarragon, salt and pepper.

6. Bring to a rolling boil and whisk in cornstarch and water solution.

7. Reduce to a gentle simmer and whisk in the butter one piece at a time until sauce thickens to a consistency thick enough to coat a spoon.

8. Set aside.

Cook Time	Temperature
Sauté onion, carrot, and celery	Medium-high for 5-6 min
Boil lobster	High for 5-10 min
Sauté shallot, garlic, and peppercorn	Medium-low for 5-7 min
Deglaze pan with brandy	Medium-high for 3-5 min
Add lobster stock and reduce	Medium-high for 5-10 min
Whisk in tomato paste and cream	Medium for 3-5 min
Whisk in butter	Medium for 3-5 min
Total	29-48 min

green beans (haricots vert)

My friend, the French chef, tells the story of going to a US supermarket in search of haricots vert. Of course, there are plenty of green beans, but the majority of them are large and overripe by French standards. Consequently, there he was in his chef's jacket, picking through the beans, looking for the smallest and most tender ones. Pretty soon, a few female shoppers stopped by to ask him what he was doing. Before he knew it, he had two or three women helping him find the perfect haricots vert. There must have been something about the charm of the French accent and the nicely starched chef's jacket.

Ingredients

1 pound fresh green beans, the smaller the better (while these can be found at every US market, Costco sells the perfect haricots vert, beautifully packaged and cleaned)

1 small shallot, diced

3 tablespoons olive oil

Salt and pepper to taste

Cookware Needed

10 or 12 inch sauté (or frying) pan

Serves 8 People as Tasting Menu

As with many things in life there is an easy way and a better way…

The Easy Way

Precook the beans in the microwave with a little water until just tender or, as the Italian say, al dente (firm to the tooth or bite).

The Better Way

Blanch the beans in boiling salted water for a few minutes then put them into an ice-water bath to chill. This will produce a vibrant green color and wonderful texture.

Final Prep

1. In a large sauté pan, sauté shallot slices in olive oil under low heat until the shallot is translucent.

2. Add the beans to warm them up, tossing to incorporate the oil and shallot flavor.

3. Add salt and pepper.

4. Serve.

Cook Time	Temperature
Option A: Blanch in salted boiling water	Medium-high for 3-4 min
Option B: Microwave	High for 3 min
Sauté shallots	Medium-low for 3-5 min
Sauté/green beans with shallot	Medium-low for 3-5 min
Total	**9-14 min**

Step	Prep Time
Prep beans	3-5 min
Dice shallot	3-5 min
Prep asparagus, peel/dice shallot	4-6 min
Total	**10-16 min**

rice

Ingredients

**1 cup rice
(I use sushi rice
quite often but
any type works)**

Follow the instructions on the package.

rack of lamb provençal

Someone once asked me, "Of the dishes you make, which is your favorite?" Here it is. There is something about a rack of lamb that is just special. With this said, lamb is a polarizing flavor. Some people like it and some people don't.

My friend Lucien and I once had a dinner party for 20 people. Of the twenty, there were at least five who fell into the category of those that don't like lamb. Lucien made a rack of lamb that night that had the "haters" fighting over the last few chops. I still have this vision of the group politely positioning themselves around the buffet, trying to get another chop. Priceless!

Done right, there is nothing quite as good and elegant as a rack of lamb. Not done right, this meat can bring the haters out. My experience has been that getting it right is predicated on two things: cooking the lamb under very high heat, and cooking it to a perfect medium rare.

The following recipe is a little different from traditional versions, but the results are fantastic.

Ingredients

1 clove garlic

½ cup fresh herbs (Italian parsley or mint or a combination of both)

Kosher salt and fresh ground pepper

Zest of one lemon

4 ½-inch slices crusty baguette

1 rack of lamb (8 chops for a tasting party of four people)

3 tablespoons Dijon mustard

1. In the bowl of a food processor fitted with a metal blade, process garlic, herbs, salt, pepper, and lemon zest until nicely ground.

2. Add pieces of baguette, broken up into 1-inch chunks.

3. Process until the crumb is the consistency of rice and the herb mixture is nicely incorporated.

4. Set aside.

5. Place a cast iron skillet on an outdoor gas grill, close the lid, and preheat it to get it as hot as you can, 400–600°F.

6. Preheat indoor broiler to high.

Cookware Needed

Food processor

Gas grill

Baking sheet

Oven broiler

Cast iron skillet

Two 10 or 12 inch sauté (or frying) pans

Serves 8 People as Tasting Menu

Step	Prep Time
Prep breadcrumbs	5-10 min
Prep rack of lamb	5-10 min
Final assembly and presentation	5-10 min
Total	**15-30 min**

7. Trim the excess fat off of the rack of lamb and wrap the bone ends in aluminum foil to protect them from the high heat on the grill.

8. Liberally sprinkle the lamb with salt and pepper.

9. Place the lamb meat-side down on the preheated cast iron skillet on the grill.

10. Close lid and cook for 2–4 minutes until you get a good sear on the hero side of the lamb.

11. Flip the lamb to bone-side down, close the lid, and cook until your instant read thermometer reads 120°F.

12. You can take it out and test the middle of one rack with a knife to make sure it is between rare and medium rare. If it needs a little more time, put it back. Be careful not to overcook. Rare is better because you can always cook it a little longer.

13. Take the racks off the grill, transfer them to a baking sheet, and spread the Dijon mustard all over the lamb meat. Press on the herb mixture, shaking off any excess.

14. Place the herb-crusted lamb under the broiler and cook for a few minutes, until the crust is golden brown.

15. Take the lamb out of the oven and let it rest for 10 minutes.

Cook Time	Temperature
Preheat grill and cast iron skillet	500°F+ for 10-15 min
Sear lamb, flesh side down	High for 3-5 min
Roast lamb, bone side down	High for 7-8 min
Finish lamb and crumb, bone side down	High for 2-3 min
Total	**15-30 min**

pommes frites (a.k.a. french fries)

See more about fryers on page 69

If you asked my friends and family what the best thing I make is, they would probably say my French fries, or as my buddy Joe calls them the "Curly Fries."

My history with fries goes way back. My mom used to make them on the stove top with an old (and very dangerous) fryer. We always loved them, but she never could get them consistently crunchy. She would make them in batches of which there were never enough. She had quite a few theories on why they were not crunchy every time. One was the oil and she even tried to save old oil under the theory that it added flavor. Mom is very bright and a great cook, but fries were never her forte. Her son has figured it out and here is the secret:

You have to cook the fries multiple times.

Growing up, McDonalds was always the gold standard for fries. I went to France while I was in high school and was amazed that the fries in France were even better than McDonalds. How do they do it? The answer in France and at McDonalds is to precook the fries. McDonalds precooks them and then freezes them, a method that works really well at home and saves time on the day of the meal. The other way is to cook them in a fryer until they just begin to show color. Let them cool before flash frying them in a very hot fryer to crisp them up.

The term "Curly Fries" comes in when I loosen up the precooked fries to make sure that they don't cling together. The loosening up ensures that the oil gets to a larger surface area on the fries and also gives them a little shape.

Ingredients
1 pound russet potatoes
Peanut oil for frying
Kosher salt

1. Wash the potatoes with cold water, making sure all dirt and grit is removed.

2. With a mandoline fitted with a ¼-inch slotted blade, cut the potatoes into long strips.

3. Place the raw potato strips into a pot of cold water.

4. In a fryer, preheat the oil to 375°F. Instant read thermometers are great but in a pinch, you can test heat by throwing one fry in the oil. If it starts a vigorous bubbling, the oil is hot enough.

Cookware Needed

**Large bowl
(filled with cold water)**

Deep fryer or large pot

Fire extinguisher

Serves 8 People as Tasting Menu

Step	Prep Time
Prep potatoes	2-3 min
Cut with mandoline	5-10 min
Total	**7-13 min**

5. When you are ready to cook, take the fries out of the water and dry them well. I use a salad spinner to get as much water out as possible, but you can also dry them on cloth or paper towels.

6. Place as many fries in the frying basket as you can while getting good coverage with oil but not overcrowding the fryer.

7. Cook the fries in batches until they just begin to show color. Drain and cool on paper towels. Repeat with the next batches.

8. While you are letting the perfectly medium rare rack of lamb rest, get your oil temperature back up to 375–400°F.

9. Again, get as many of your precooked fries into the basket while getting good coverage with oil but not overcrowding the fryer.

10. Cook the fries until they turn a dark golden brown. You can even cook them a few times, pulling the basket out, letting the temperature of the oil come back up then cooking them again.

11. When you get them to that crunchy crisp texture you love, pull them out, let them drain, hit them with a good dose of Kosher salt and serve.

12. WARNING: Watch out French fry poachers. You know the type. They hang around the kitchen under the guise of "wanting to help." If you don't keep an eye on them, they will poach 50% of your fries before you get the first dish plated.

Cook Time	Temperature
Precook potatoes	325°F for 5-7 min
Cool potatoes	8-10 min
Finish potatoes	375°F for 5-7 min
Total	**18-24 min**

asparagus

Ingredients

1 pound asparagus
(the smaller the better)

1 small shallot, diced

3 tablespoons olive oil

Salt and pepper to taste

Cookware Needed

Baking sheet

Serves 8 People
as Tasting Menu

As with the green beans there is an easy way and a better way…

The Easy Way

Precook the asparagus in the microwave with a little water until just tender to the tooth.

The Better Way

Blanch the asparagus in boiling salted water for a few minutes then put them into an ice-water bath to chill. This will produce a vibrant green color and wonderful texture.

Final Prep

1. In a large sauté pan, sauté the shallot in olive oil under low heat until the shallot is translucent.

2. Add the asparagus to warm them up, tossing to incorporate the oil and shallot flavor.

3. Add salt and pepper.

4. Serve.

Step	Prep Time
Prep asparagus, peel/dice shallot	4-6 min
Total	**4-6 min**

Cook Time	Temperature
Roast asparagus	380°F for 15-20 min
Total	**15-20 min**

béarnaise blush sauce

Ingredients

One packet Knorr or McCormick béarnaise sauce, prepared following the package instructions (with milk and butter as required)

2 tablespoons tomato paste

Cookware Needed

Medium sauce pot

Wire whisk

Serves 8 People as Tasting Menu

1. Prepare the béarnaise sauce as instructed on the package.

2. Whisk in the tomato paste to give it the blush color.

Step	Prep Time
Prep sauce (following package instructions)	2-3 min
Prep beef	5-10 min
Total	**13-23 min**

Cook Time	Temperature
Cook sauce (following package instructions)	High for 8-10 min
Finish by whisking in tomato paste	High for 3-5 min
Total	**18-24 min**

cake parfaits

I am not a big dessert guy. Baking is just not my thing. I do believe, though, that you need dessert to complement a nice meal. In looking for a way to deliver a great dessert with minimal effort, the restaurant trend to mini desserts makes a lot of sense. I particularly like the idea of delivering lots of options with little work.

Ingredients

A few slices of carrot cake (most supermarkets sell smaller portions of cake in their bakery sections)

A few slices of German chocolate cake*

1 can of Reddi Wip

Fresh berries

Lime for zesting

Sprigs of mint (one per parfait)

Cookware Needed

Fluted Champagne glass (or any small glass)

Serves 8 People as Tasting Menu

1 Crush each cake slice in a small bowl with a fork.

2. Spoon one cake mixture into a fluted champagne glass (or any small glass—this is a great place to use those shot glasses you stole in college), about ⅓ full.

3. Squirt on the Reddi Wip.

4. Top with berries, mint sprig and lime zest.

5. You can make one of each for everyone or just let people fight over them.

*Many of today's big products started by filling a need for a popular recipe. These "Hero recipes" have historically been a huge seller behind many brands. In the old General Foods world, it was said that the recipe for German Chocolate cake was the single most asked-for recipe. Needless to say, that recipe was a big seller for Baker's German Chocolate Bars and Baker's coconut.

Step	Prep Time
Prep cake	3-5 min
Assemble parfaits	5-10 min
Total	**8-15 min**

Prep Schedule—Mise en Place (for a Saturday evening dinner)
Thursday
Make lobster stock
Friday
Make croutons and parfait minis
Saturday
10:00AM	Make tomato/olive mixture
11:00	Dice/sauté bacon
12:00PM	Prep cod
1:00	Make vinaigrette
3:00	Prep and precook pommes frites
4:00	Prep asparagus
4:10	Prep green beans
5:00	Make Sauce Americaine
5:10	Prep and precook rack of lamb
5:20	Make Béarnaise blush sauce*
6:00	Make rice
6:10	Prep bacon and assemble stuffed shrimp
6:20	Grill/roast shrimp
6:30	Roast asparagus
6:35	Sauté green beans
6:45	Sauté/roast cod
7:00	Assemble and lay out romaine wedges
7:10	Guests arrive, serve wine
7:30	Assemble and serve romaine wedges
7:40	Roast cod in oven
7:50	Finish and serve rack of lamb
8:00	Assemble and serve lamb, rice and beans
9:00	Finish and serve dessert

* Sauces can be made up to a week in advance.

Menu Example

The following Saturday Night Menu works well for a Classic Supper Club dinner.

Saturday Night Menu

Hors d'Oeuvres

Gorgonzola and walnut enrobed Grapes

First Course

Romaine wedges with blue cheese vinaigrette, bacon, heirloom tomatoes and homemade croutons

Main Course

Rack of Lamb Provençal

Pommes Macaire

Salsa Verde

Sautéed Chanterelles

Haricots Vert with shallot and pine nuts

Dessert

Cookie balls with fresh raspberries and Grand Marnier

Wine Recommendations

Wine	Origin	Composition	Price
Red			
Saldo Zinfandel	California	Zinfandel	$35.99
Gallo Signature Series Cabernet Sauvignon	Napa Valley CA	Cabernet Sauvignon	$34.99
Elk Cove Pinot Noir	Willamette Valley OR	Pinot Noir	$29.99
White			
Crème de lys Chardonnay	CA Central Coast	Chardonnay	$12.00
Massimo Sauvignon Blanc	New Zealand	Sauvignon Blanc	$13.95
Remy Pannier Vouvray	Loire France	Vouray	$17.89

gorgonzola and walnut enrobed grapes

Ingredients

6 ounces crumbled Gorgonzola cheese (can also use blue cheese)

4 ounces cream cheese

1 cup finely chopped walnuts

20 seedless red grapes

Cookware Needed

Mixing bowl

Baking sheet

Serves 8 People

1. Leave the Gorgonzola and cream cheeses out at room temperature for at least an hour to soften.

2. Preheat oven to 325°F. On a cookie sheet, spread out the chopped walnuts and toast for five minutes. Remove and allow to cool.

3. Using a wooden spoon (or electric mixer), cream together the Gorgonzola and cream cheeses.

4. Put one tablespoon of the cheese mixture in the palm of your hand. Embed one grape in this mixture, shaping the mixture around the grape to coat.

5. Roll the covered grape in the walnuts before placing on a serving tray.

6. Chill for 30 minutes until coating is firm.

7. If grapes are large, use a sharp knife to cut into halves.

Step	Prep Time
Chop walnuts	3-5 min
Combine Gorgonzola and cream cheese	4-6 min
Enrobe grapes	10-25 min
Chill enrobed grapes	30-30 min
Total	**47-56 min**

Cook Time	Temperature
Soften cream cheese in microwave	High for ½-1 min
Toast walnuts	325°F for 4-6 min
Total	**4½-7 min**

romaine wedge with gorgonzola vinaigrette

There are six components that should be made in advance and assembled right before being served:

1. Vinaigrette
2. Croutons
3. Tomato/olive mix
4. Bacon
5. Onion rings
6. Romaine wedges

Ingredients

6 cloves garlic, finely diced with 2 teaspoons Kosher Salt

2 heaping tablespoons Dijon mustard

3 tablespoons white wine vinegar

Juice of one lemon

2 teaspoons honey

1 cup extra virgin olive oil

2 tablespoons Italian parsley, finely chopped

2 cups roughly grated Gorgonzola cheese

Cookware Needed

Mixing bowl

Wire whisk

Serves 8 People as Tasting Menu

1. In a large mixing bowl add garlic, mustard, vinegar, lemon juice and honey.

2. Whisk together then drizzle in the olive oil, whisking vigorously. Keep whisking until the vinaigrette is nicely emulsified.

3. Whisk in the Italian parsley and Gorgonzola. (Note: The Gorgonzola can be added at the last minute. You should ask if everyone likes Gorgonzola cheese as some people are allergic to it.)

4. Set aside or refrigerate.

Step	Prep Time
Dice/mash garlic	3–5 min
Chop parsley	2–3 min
Grate Gorgonzola	3–4 min
Whisk	3–5 min
Total	**47-56 min**

romaine wedge

Ingredients

Romaine hearts (I prefer the artisan hearts that are trimmed and cleaned)

1 pound Oscar Mayer bacon, cut into 1-inch pieces

1 small package (1 pint) grape tomatoes, cut into halves

24 pitted Kalamata olives

3 green onions, roughly chopped into ¼-inch pieces

2 cloves garlic, cut into paper-thin slices

3 tablespoons olive oil

16 rings red onion, thinly sliced and separated

Kosher salt and freshly ground pepper to taste

1. Trim romaine hearts to 8 inches in length. Cut into quarters lengthwise. Cover with a damp paper towel and set aside.

2. Brown the bacon. Set aside. (Don't pick.)

3. In a mixing bowl combine tomatoes, olives, green onion, garlic, olive oil, salt and pepper. Mix and set aside.

4. Set aside red onion.

Cookware Needed

Mixing bowl

Wire whisk

10 or 12 inch sauté (or frying) pans

Serves 8 People as Tasting Menu

Cook Time	Temperature
Sauté bacon	Medium for 7-10 min
Total	**15-20 min**

Step	Prep Time
Trim/quarter romaine	3–5 min
Dice bacon	2–3 min
Mix tomato/olive mixture	2–3 min
Final assembly and presentation	5–10 min
Total	**47-56 min**

croutons

Ingredients

7 cloves garlic, finely chopped

¼ cup unsalted butter

¼–½ cup olive oil

**½ French baguette,
cut into 1 × 1 inch pieces**

Cookware Needed

**10 or 12 inch sauté
(or frying) pans**

Serves 8 People
as Tasting Menu

Step	Prep Time
Chop garlic	2–3 min
Cut baguette	3–4 min
Total	**5-7 min**

1. Preheat oven to 380°F.

2. In a large sauté pan on the stovetop, sauté garlic in butter and ¼ cup olive oil for 4 minutes under medium/low heat until garlic softens.

3. Add baguette pieces and stir so that they are coated in olive oil (add a little more oil if necessary) under high heat.

4. When the bread starts to brown, shift the sauté pan into the oven.

5. Cook in the oven for 5–10 minutes or until the croutons are crunchy brown.

Final Prep/Plating

6. Place Romaine quarters onto full size plates.

7. Drizzle liberally with Gorgonzola Vinaigrette.

8. Add tomato/olive mixture.

9. Add croutons and bacon.

10. Top with red onion rings.

11. Serve.

Cook Time	Temperature
Sauté garlic	Low for 4-5 min
Sauté bread, garlic and oil	Medium-high for 5-6 min
Bake croutons	380°F for 5-10 min
Total	**14-21 min**

Fryers

Having the right fryer makes it easy, but there are all kinds of options:

- Pot on the stove with a wire basket, slotted spoon or Asian wire skimmer
- Electric fryers: "Fry Daddy's" or "Fry Babies" (safest option)
- Propane fueled "Turkey Fryers" fitted with 8-inch by 20-inch fry pot. This is my fryer of choice because you can get quantity and quality but they are risky…

My son learned at an early age that cooking for girls helped his popularity. He hosted parties at the house, where he made French fries when his parents were home with no problem. Of course his dad warned him about using the turkey fryer and the dangers of oil and open flame. Then one spring, my wife and I were out in California for our niece's college graduation and got a call from Brian with: "Dad what do I do? The oil boiled over and caught on fire." I told him to use the fire extinguisher. He said, "We did but the flame keeps coming back." I said, "Call 911." While he was trying to get the fire department, one buddy got the flame out with the fire extinguisher and a second doused the fryer with a garden hose. Miraculously, with the exception of a few burn marks on our patio, we had no injuries or damage.

The morals of this story are:

- If you are going to use an open-flamed fryer, make sure it is outside and you have a good-sized fire extinguisher.
- One good way to teach your children to be careful with open flames and oil is to have them experience a little oil fire. Poor Brian has been scarred for life. For years he has wanted no part of making French fries. Ten years later, he did make fries at a tailgating event, but trust me, he was careful.

rack of lamb provençal

Someone once asked me, "Of the dishes you make, which is your favorite?" Here it is. There is something about a rack of lamb that is just special. With this said, lamb is a polarizing flavor. Some people like it and some don't.

My friend, Lucien, and I once had a dinner party for 20 people. Of the twenty, there were at least five who fell into the category of those that don't like lamb. Lucien made a rack of lamb that night that had the "haters" fighting over the last few chops. I still have this vision of the group politely positioning themselves around the buffet, trying to get another chop. Priceless!

Done right, there is nothing quite as good and elegant as a rack of lamb. Not done right, this meat can bring the haters out. My experience has been that getting it right is predicated on two things:

- Cooking the lamb under very high heat, and
- Cooking it to a perfect medium rare.

The following recipe is a little different from traditional versions, but the results are fantastic.

Ingredients

2 rack of lamb (2 chops per person for a tasting party, 4 chops per person for a regular main course)

½ cup fresh herbs (Italian parsley or mint or a combination of both)

1 clove garlic

Zest of one lemon

Kosher salt and fresh ground pepper

6 ½-inch slices crusty baguette

4 tablespoons Dijon mustard

1. In the bowl of a food processor fitted with a metal blade, place the herbs, garlic, salt, pepper, and lemon zest. Process until nicely ground.

2. Break bread into small chunks and add. Process until the crumb is the consistency of rice and the herb mixture is nicely incorporated.

3. Set aside.

4. Place a cast iron skillet on your gas grill, close the lid and preheat it to get it as hot as you can. Target 400–600°F.

5. Preheat your broiler back in the kitchen to high.

Cookware Needed

Food processor

Gas grill

Baking sheet

Oven broiler

Cast iron skillet

Serves 8 People

Step	Prep Time
Prep breadcrumbs	5–10
Prep rack of lamb	5–10
Final assembly and presentation	5–10
Total	**15-30 min**

Cook Time	Temp
Preheat grill /cast iron skillet	500°F+ for 10-15 min
Sear lamb, flesh side down	High for 3-5 min
Roast lamb, bone side down	High for 7-8 min
Finish lamb and crumb, bone side down	High for 2-3 min
Total	**22-31 min**

6. Trim the excess fat off of the rack of lamb and wrap the bone ends in aluminum foil to protect them from the high heat on the grill.

7. Liberally sprinkle the lamb with salt and pepper.

8. Place an external read thermometer into the center of the lamb.

9. Place the lamb meat-side down on the preheated cast iron skillet on the grill.

10. Close the lid and cook for 2–4 minutes until you get a good sear on the hero side (the one you want to look the best) of the lamb.

11. Flip the lamb to bone-side down, close the lid and cook until the instant read thermometer reads 120°F. I also test doneness by touch. Uncooked meat is really soft. Overcooked meat is hard. I keep touching as it cooks. As the meat starts to firm up, you are moving from rare to medium. The key is practice, practice, practice.

12. Pull the lamb out and test the middle of one rack with a knife to make sure it is between rare and medium rare. If it needs a little more, put it back. But be careful not to overcook. Rare is better because you can always cook it a little longer.

13. Take the racks off the grill, transfer them to a baking sheet and spread the Dijon mustard all over the lamb meat. Press on the herb mixture, shaking off any excess.

14. Place the herb-crusted lamb under the broiler and cook for a few minutes until the crust is golden brown.

15. Take the lamb out of the oven and let it rest for 10 minutes.

pommes macaire (a.k.a. potato casserole)

Ingredients

2 pounds russet potatoes

2 tablespoons olive oil

1 large onion, diced

1 stick butter

½ cup heavy cream

2 tablespoons kosher salt

½ pound bacon, cut into ½-inch dice

2 large eggs

1 cup Gruyère cheese, grated

2 cups Parmesan cheese, coarsely grated

4 green onions, cut into a ¼-inch dice (both white and green parts)

Kosher salt and pepper to taste

Cookware Needed

9 × 13 baking dish

Baking sheet

Mixing bowl

10 or 12 inch sauté (or frying) pan

Serves 8 People

1. Clean the potatoes under cold running water then pat dry with a paper towel. Brush with olive oil and liberally sprinkle with kosher salt. Place on a baking sheet in a preheated 380°F oven for 1 hour or until the potatoes are fork-tender. Take out of the oven and let cool.

2 In a medium skillet, sauté the bacon until browned. Set aside.

3. In the same skillet drain some of the bacon fat, leaving enough to liberally coat the bottom of the pan. Sauté the onion under low heat until it just starts to brown.

4. Melt butter in a microwave.

5. Scramble the eggs with heavy cream.

6. Peel the potatoes then coarsely mash, leaving them still a little chunky. Be careful not overmash, as doing so breaks down the starch.

7. In a large mixing bowl, mix the potatoes, egg/cream, butter, onion, bacon, Gruyère and 1 cup of Parmesan.

8. Place in a 9 ×13 baking dish and top with the remaining Parmesan.

9. Bake in 380°F preheated over for 30 minutes or until the top is a deep golden brown.

10. Top with green onion.

11. While this dish can be served as a casserole, I prefer to let it cool, cut it into 3-inch triangles and reheat it in the oven for 5–10 minutes before plating.

Cook Time	Temperature
Bake potatoes	380°F for 60–70 min
Sauté bacon	Medium-high for 7-10 min
Sauté onion	Medium-high for 7-10 min
Melt butter in microwave	High for 2-3 min
Bake potato mixture	380ºF for 30-40 min
Total	**106-133 min**

Step	Prep Time
Prep potatoes	3–5 min
Prep bacon, onion and cheese	5–10 min
Scramble eggs	3–5 min
Cool potatoes	30–40 min
Peel and mash potatoes	5–10 min
Final assembly and presentation	5–10
Total	**51-80 min**

sautéed chanterelles

Ingredients

3 tablespoons butter

10 ounces chanterelle mushrooms, cleaned

Salt and pepper

Cookware Needed

9 × 13 baking dish

Baking sheet

Mixing bowl

10 or 12 inch sauté (or frying) pan

Serves 8 People

1. In a large sauté pan, melt the butter and add mushrooms. Sauté for 10–15 minutes, stirring occasionally.

2. Season with salt and pepper.

3. Serve.

Cook Time	Temperature
Sauté mushrooms	Medium-high for 10-15 min
Total	**10-15 min**

Step	Prep Time
Prep mushrooms	3–5 min
Total	**3-5 min**

salsa verde

Ingredients

1 large shallot, minced (½ cup)

¼ cup plus 2 tablespoons extra virgin olive oil

2 cups tightly pressed fresh herbs (Italian parsley, mint, chives, green onion, fresh oregano, etc.—any one or any combination)

2 tablespoons Dijon mustard

Salt and pepper to taste

Cookware Needed

Food processor

10 or 12 inch sauté (or frying) pan

Serves 8 People

1. In a sauté pan, sauté shallot under low heat in 2 tablespoons of olive oil until shallot is translucent. Let cool in the pan for 5–10 minutes.

2. Into a food processor fitted with a steel blade, put shallot, herbs, mustard, remaining olive oil, salt and pepper.

3. Pulse to incorporate then set aside

Step	Prep Time
Prep shallots/herbs	3–5
Cool shallots	5–10
Combine in food processor	1–2
Total	**9-17 min**

Cook Time	Temperature
Sauté shallot	Medium-low for 5-7 min
Total	**5-7 min**

haricots vert

Ingredients

1 pound green beans
(the smaller the better)

1 small shallot, diced

3 tablespoons olive oil

Salt and pepper to taste

Cookware Needed

10 or 12 inch sauté
(or frying) pan

Serves 8 People
as Tasting Menu

Step	Prep Time
Prep beans	3–5
Dice shallots	3–5
Total	**6-10 min**

The Easy Way

Precook the beans in the microwave with a little water until just tender to the tooth (about 3 minutes).

The Better Way

Blanch the beans in boiling salted water for a few minutes then put them into an ice-water bath to chill. This will produce a vibrant green color and wonderful texture.

Final Prep

1. In a large sauté pan, sauté the shallot in olive oil under low heat until the shallot is translucent.

2. Add the beans to warm them up. Toss to incorporate the oil/shallot flavor.

3. Add salt and pepper and serve.

Cook Time	Temperature
Option A: Blanch in salted boiling water	Medium-high for 3-4 min
Option B: Microwave	High for 3-3 minutes
Sauté shallots	Medium-low for 3-5 min
Sauté green beans with shallots	Medium-low for 3-5 min
Total	**5-7 min**

fresh raspberries infused with grand marnier

Ingredients

1 cup water

1 cup sugar

1 small package fresh raspberries

2 ounces Grand Marnier

Cookware Needed

Small saucepan

Mixing bowl

Serves 8 People

1. Make a simple syrup by combining water and sugar in a small saucepan. Heat and whisk until the sugar dissolves.

2. Add Grand Marnier. Let cool.

3. Mix in raspberries.

Step	Prep Time
Prep berries	3–5 min
Combine/cool syrup	5–10 min
Final prep	3–5 min
Total	**11-20 min**

Cook Time	Temperature
Make simple syrup	Medium for 5-10 min
Total	**5-7 min**

cookie balls

Ingredients

¼ cup butter, softened

¾ cup brown sugar, tightly packed

1 egg

1⅓ cup all-purpose flour

1 cup Baker's Angel Flake coconut*

6 ounces semisweet chocolate chips

Cookware Needed

Mixing bowl

Baking sheet

Serves 8 People

Step	Prep Time
Prep cookie dough	5-10 min
Total	5-10 min

1. Preheat oven to 375°F.

2. In a large mixing bowl, mix butter, sugar and egg.

3. Stir in flour, coconut and chocolate chips.

4. Take 1 heaping teaspoon of the mixture and roll in your hands to make a ball.

5. Place on an ungreased baking sheet.

6. Bake for about 10 minutes or until lightly browned.

Cook Time	Temperature
Bake cookies	375°F for 8-12 min
Total	8.12 min

*This may sound like an infomercial, but coconut is something I know way too much about. I ran the Franklin Baker Coconut Company in the Philippines for 15 years. One thing about coconut is that it comes from a tropical environment that is susceptible to microbiological contamination. Salmonella can be a big problem. I recommend Baker's coconut because I know Baker's uses a proprietary pasteurization process to ensure product safety. Beyond this, it has been said that on my tombstone it will say, "He knew coconut."

Prep Schedule—Mise en Place (for a Saturday evening dinner)
Thursday
Make Pommes Macaire
Friday
Make croutons and enrobed grapes
Saturday
10:00AM Make tomato/olive mixture
11:00   Dice and sauté bacon
12:00PM Prep cod
1:00   Make vinaigrette
3:00   Cut and stage Pommes Macaire
4:00   Prep haricots vert
4:10   Make Salsa Verde
5:10   Prep and precook rack of lamb
6:20   Prep Romaine wedges
6:30   Warm Pommes Macaire
6:35   Sauté haricots vert
6:45   Sauté chanterelles
7:00   Assemble and lay out romaine wedges
7:10   Guests arrive, serve wine
7:15   Chit chat
7:30   Assemble and serve romaine wedges
7:40   Grill rack of lamb
7:50   Finish and serve rack of lamb
8:00   Assemble and serve lamb, pommes and beans
9:00   Finish and serve dessert

> * Sauces can be made up to a week in advance.

Wine Recommendations

Wine	Origin	Composition	Price
Red			
Phelps Cabernet	Napa, CA	Cabernet Sauvignon	$60.00
Pendulum Red Blend	Columbia Valley, OR	Red Blend	$15.00
Youngberg Hill Oregon Pinot Noir	Willamette Valley OR	Pinot Noir	$99.00
White			
Folie a Deux Chardonnay	Sonoma County, CA	Chardonnay	$10.00
Robert Mondavi Fume Blanc	Napa Valley, CA	Sauvignon Blanc	$14.99
Atemms Pinot Grigio Ramato	Venezia Guilia, Italia	Pinot Grigio	$12.25

Chapter 4

Impromptu Friday Nights

Not all supper clubs have to be formal and structured. There is something special about the spontaneity of an event that is organized at the last minute. Usually, the result is a lot of fun.

The Impromptu Friday Night Club is patterned after a group of friends who would get together on a Friday night with minimal notice and prep time. The genesis goes back to when I worked with chef Lucien Vendome at Kraft Food Ingredients. Lucien would stop by my office at 3 pm on a Friday afternoon and ask, "Are you in town this weekend?" (Code for: What are you doing tonight?) I would respond with, "The usual suspects?" From there, I would check with the "War Department" (a.k.a. my wife, Susan). With her permission, Lucien and I would develop the menu.

There are four significant elements to a successful impromptu supper club:

1. Spontaneity. Spontaneity is one of the biggest keys to this type of club. It is always just a little more fun when you don't expect it.

2. Control. One of the nice things about this club is that the host gets to control the dinner. Of course, with control comes a big piece

of the work. One of the beauties of our Impromptu Friday Nights was that I had another chef to help with the preparation. Lucien is a culinary genius and would take the lead in menu development as well as preparation. It took more than a few dinners for Lucien and I to get comfortable cooking together. I started out with the premise that when it was in my kitchen I would be the cook and Lucien the guest. That didn't work. For one thing Lucien is one of the most knowledgeable and innovative chefs in the world. The other thing is that he just enjoys the work. Over time we got comfortable working together in my kitchen, and the results were some of the best evenings imaginable.

3. Flexibility. Having a flexible spouse/partner/roommate is crucial. For example, telling your wife at 3 pm that you are having 10 people over for dinner at 7 pm can be intimidating. Susan rarely vetoes the idea. Her main caveat is always, "Is the house clean?"

4. "The Usual Suspects." It has always amazed me that we could call four other couples at 4 pm on a Friday and get them to show up at 7 pm. There was something serendipitous about this group and the event. At the time, we all lived in the same neighborhood and worked in Memphis. The guys all traveled extensively for work, which made scheduling anything with them difficult. Maybe it was because we did it on Friday nights, which were less busy. Or maybe it was because the food was good and we had a lot of fun. But nine out of ten times that we had one of these dinners, everyone invited would somehow make it.

Menu Development

Given the time frame involved, you have to keep the menu simple. Lucien and I would typically spend 10 minutes scratching out a menu based on:

- A current theme, e.g., Italian food we had experienced in Chicago the month before.
- What is available in the local market. We worked across the street from a Costco, so our protein usually came from there. Seasonal produce was always a major factor.

- Dishes with minimal prep time. Our menu would more than likely be made up of items that could be made "à la minute" one of Lucien's favorite expressions, meaning "at the last minute").

Cost

The reality of the Impromptu Friday Night is that the bulk of the expense falls to the host. One of the beauties of paying for things is that you are able to better control those things.

As it turns out, the "Usual Suspects" in my Impromptu Friday Night club have very good tastes in wine. When we would call to invite people, they would always ask, "What can we bring?" The simple answer was to ask them to bring wine.

Another approach is to keep track of costs and divide the expense up at the end of the night. The "divide and conquer" approach works very well with the more formal supper club approach outlined earlier. Some people might think that my approach of absorbing the cost as being overly gracious. Susan, who knows me better than anyone, would tell you the truth is that for me, the price of control is worth it.

Mise en Place

If your guests are arriving at 7 pm, you should begin your meal prep at 6 pm (make crudités earlier, if possible). Time is of the essence. Using the following menu, I will give you an example of the preparation process for an impromptu dinner with eight people.

Friday Night Menu
    Hors d'Oeuvres
    Crudité with Tapenade
    First Course
    Roasted Red Bell Pepper with Buffalo Mozzarella and Fresh Basil
    Main Course
    Chicken Milanese with Salsa Verde
    Pasta with Sausage, Olive Oil, Garlic and Fresh Herbs
    Baked Escarole
    Dessert
    Vanilla Ice Cream
    Berries and Grand Marnier Sauce

crudités with tapenade

Crudités Ingredients
2–3 celery stalks
1½ cups baby carrots

Tapenade Ingredients
4 ounces pitted Kalamata olives
4 ounces sundried tomatoes in oil
4 ounces roasted garlic
Salt and pepper to taste

Cookware Needed
Food processor

Serves 8 People

Crudités

1. Clean celery and cut into 1½-inch pieces.

2. Arrange celery and carrots on a serving plate.

Tapenade

1. Combine olives, tomatoes and garlic in a food processor. Add salt and pepper.

2. Pulse the processor until your tapenade is the right consistency. (I like it a little chunky so you know what you are eating. If it is too chunky, add a few tablespoons of olive oil..

3. You can plate and serve right away or cover in plastic wrap and put it in the refrigerator until it is time to serve.

Step	Prep Time
Prep celery and carrots	3–5 min
Final prep	2–4 min
Combine ingredients in food processor	1–2 min
Total	11-20 min

roasted red bell pepper with buffalo mozzarella and fresh basil

Ingredients

2 large red bell peppers

4 cloves garlic, sliced paper thin

2 medium sized balls buffalo mozzarella

10 basil leaves

¼ cup extra virgin olive oil

2 tablespoons balsamic vinegar

Kosher salt and pepper

Cookware Needed

Gas grill

Paper bag or sealable container

10 or 12 inch sauté (or frying) pans

Serves 8 People

1. Roast the red bell peppers on a gas grill. Char all sides so that the outside is blackened.

2. Place the charred peppers in a brown paper bag (or a sealable plastic container) and wrap the top tightly to seal. Allow the peppers to steam and cool for 15–20 minutes. This process allows the skin to separate from the body of the pepper.

3. Take the cooled pepper out of the bag. Remove the stem and core with a knife and then cut into quarters. Scrape the charred skin off the outside and the seeds and pieces of core from the inside. Place in a bowl.

4. Sauté garlic slices in olive oil under very low heat for 5 minutes. Pour the oil/garlic on the peppers. Let peppers marinate for at least 30 minutes.

5. Arrange peppers in the middle of a good-sized serving plate. Place slices of mozzarella in the middle. Add fresh basil leaves.

6. Drizzle with some of the oil used to marinate the peppers and balsamic vinegar. Add salt and pepper to taste. Serve.

Step	Prep Time
Peel, trim and quarter peppers	3–5 min
Final assembly and presentation	5–10 min
Total	**8-15 min**

Cook Time	Temperature
Roast peppers on grill	High for 10-15 min
Cool charred peppers in a bag	
Sauté garlic	Medium-low for 5-6 min
Marinate peppers in garlic and oil	10-15 min
Sauté bacon	Medium for 7-10
Total	**5-7 min**

pasta with sausage, olive oil, garlic and fresh herbs

Ingredients

½ pound pasta (a mini penne works very well)

1 cup extra virgin olive oil*

8 ounces sweet Italian sausage, cut into ½-in pieces

7 cloves garlic, peeled and sliced Goodfellas† thin

1 cup fresh basil, chopped

1 cup Italian parsley, chopped

1 cup fresh Romano cheese, grated

Cookware Needed

Large sauce pot

10 or 12 inch sauté (or frying) pans

Serves 8 People

1. Boil pasta following the instructions on the package. When cooked, drain and toss with a few tablespoons of olive oil. Set aside.

2. In a nonstick pan, sauté sausage until cooked through (about 8 minutes). Set aside.

3. Sauté garlic in ¾ cup olive oil under very low heat until translucent.

4. With all of the above set aside, your pasta mise en place is ready.

Just before serving:

5. Add the pasta and sausage to olive oil/garlic in the pan. Sauté for a few minutes to heat and add texture.

5. In a large pasta bowl, combine the pasta/sausage mixture, fresh herbs and grated cheese.

7. Toss and serve.

Cook Time	Temperature
Boil water	High for 10-15 min
Sauté sausage	Medium for 7-10 min
Sauté garlic	Medium-low for 5-7 min
Cook pasta	Medium-high for 10-12 min
Reheat pasta/garlic/sausage	Medium-high for 8-10 min
Total	35-49 min

* I love olive oil. We buy extra virgin olive oil at Costco and use it liberally. While not the quality of some estate bottled brands, it works very well in a wide array of uses. My sister and I are both food snobs, but in some cases she drives me crazy. She once chastised me with, "You mean you are not using estate-bottled olive oil?" I am a trained flavor panelist. Actually, I have been trained twice while working at Kraft. From this training I know that some people have excellent palates, but most people (like me…the reason for being trained twice?) can't tell, as we said back in New York, "shit from Shinola." The best proof of this was an old test we did at Kraft. If you took the color out of 10 flavors of Jell-O, most people would be lucky to pick the correct flavor in two of the 10. Long story short, if you are cooking with an extra virgin olive oil, don't waste your money on an expensive brand.

†Remember the scene in the movie *Goodfellas* where they are cooking in prison? Paulie Cicero (Paul Sorvino) sliced his garlic with a razor blade. The razor blade might be a little much, but the thinner the garlic, the better. By getting the garlic really thin, you reduce the risk of overpowering the dish with the garlic flavor.

Step	Prep Time
Prep bacon and cheese	5–10
Make breadcrumbs in food processor	1–2
prep cheese and herbs	3–5
Combine cooked pasta, sausage and herbs	3–5
Total	**8-15 min**

chicken milanese

Ingredients

16 chicken tenderloins

Salt and pepper

8 ounces panko breadcrumbs

1 cup flour

1 egg

1 cup milk

½ teaspoon Tabasco sauce

1 cup olive oil (you may need a little more for frying)

Cookware Needed

xxx

Serves 8 People

1. Place a chicken tenderloin between two pieces of plastic wrap and pound out to ¼-inch thickness. Pound out the remainder of chicken (2 pieces per person) and set aside on a piece of wax paper. Sprinkle with salt and pepper.

2. Place panko breadcrumbs on a platter.

3. Pour flour on a separate plate and sprinkle liberally with salt and pepper.

4. In a bowl, combine egg and milk with Tabasco sauce. Beat together until incorporated.

5. Dredge one piece of chicken in flour. Dunk it in the egg wash then put it in the breadcrumbs. Turn the chicken over to make sure it is well coated with crumb. Set aside on a new sheet of wax paper.

6. Repeat the process with the remaining chicken.

7. Cover the bottom of a large frying pan with olive oil. Heat until close to smoking then sauté chicken until golden brown (about 4 minutes on each side).

8. Twenty minutes before serving, warm the chicken on a cookie sheet in a 200°F oven.

italian salsa verde

Ingredients

½ cup shallots, diced

5 cloves garlic, diced

¾ cup olive oil

1 cup fresh basil

1 cup Italian parsley

2 tablespoons Dijon mustard

1 tablespoon honey

Salt and pepper to taste

Cookware Needed

Food processor

10 or 12 inch sauté (or frying) pans

Serves 8 People

1. Sauté shallot and garlic in olive oil. Set aside to cool.

2. In a food processor, combine basil, parsley, Dijon mustard, honey and the shallot/garlic/olive oil mixture. Add salt and pepper to taste.

3. Pulse until smooth. You may have to add a few more tablespoons of olive oil to get the desired consistency.

4. Set aside in a bowl and serve at room temperature.

Step	Prep Time
Prep shallots and herbs	3–5
Cool shallots	5–10
Combine in food processor	1–2
Total	9-17 min

Cook Time	Temperature
Sauté shallot	Medium-low for 5-7 min
Total	5-7 min

baked escarole

Ingredients

6 gloves garlic,
sliced *Goodfellas*-thin

½ cup olive oil

1 large head escarole
(about 6 cups)

1 cup breadcrumbs

1 cup Parmesan cheese

Cookware Needed

Food processor

10 or 12 inch sauté
(or frying) pans

9 × 13 baking dish

Serves 8 People

1. In a large frying pan, sauté garlic in olive oil under low heat.

2. Roughly chop escarole. Add to the garlic oil and sauté for a few minutes until the escarole is slightly wilted.

3. In a large bowl, combine the escarole and garlic oil with breadcrumbs and Parmesan. Toss and place into a baking dish.

4. Bake in a 375°F oven for 25 minutes until bubbly and heated through.

Cook Time	Temperature
Wilt escarole	Medium-high for 2-3 min
Bake escarole	375°F for 25–30 min
Total	**27-33 min**

Step	Prep Time
Prep garlic and escarole	3-5 min
Total	**3-5 min**

vanilla ice cream served with fresh raspberries infused with grand marnier

Ingredients

1 cup sugar

1 cup water

2 ounces Grand Marnier

2 cups raspberries
(I love raspberries, but
you can choose any
that are in season)

Vanilla ice cream

Cookware Needed

Small saucepan

Mixing bowl

Serves 8 People

1. Make simple syrup by combining sugar and water in a pot over medium heat. Whisk until the sugar dissolves.

2. Add Grand Marnier.

3. Set aside to cool.

4. At the last minute before serving, combine with berries and serve over ice cream.

Cook Time	Temperature
Make simple syrup	Medium for 5-10 min
Total	**5-10 min**

Step	Prep Time
Prep berries	3–5 min
Combine and cool syrup	5–10 min
Final prep	3–5 min
Total	**11-20 min**

Friday Night Menu Final Prep/Plating

Your guests have arrived and you have served them a drink or two and they are enjoying the Crudités with Tapenade. The entrees can be served family style (platters), or they can be plated. I always prefer to plate as most people "eat with their eyes," and a plated meal makes a better presentation.

Where you stand:

- The chicken and escarole are warming in the oven.
- The Italian Salsa Verde is at room temperature in the food processor.
- The pasta and sausage has been tossed with herbs and cheese.

When your guests have arrived and you're ready for the main course:

1. Place the chicken on the plate.

2. Add a spoon of escarole.

3. Add a spoon of pasta.

4. Dress the plate with the Italian Salsa Verde with emphasis on the chicken.

At the table, serve each guest a plate. Have plates and bowls with extra chicken, pasta, escarole and Italian Salsa Verde. Make sure everyone has wine and water to drink.

Enjoy!

Prep Schedule—Mise en Place (for a Friday evening dinner)
Friday

5:20 PM   Prep crudités
6:00   Roast and prep peppers
6:20   Prep and sauté chicken
6:30   Prep pasta
6:35   Prep and bake escarole
6:45   Warm chicken
7:10   Guests arrive, serve wine and crudités
7:15   Chit chat
7:30   Assemble and serve peppers
7:40   Sauté pasta
8:00   Assemble and serve chicken, pasta and escarole
9:00   Finish and serve dessert

Wine Recommendations

Wine	Origin	Composition	Price
Red			
Kiona Cabernet	WA	Cabernet Sauvignon	$19.69
BV Tapestry	Napa, CA	Red Blend	$50.00
Flowers Pinot Noir	Sonoma Coast ,CA	Pinot Noir	$38.00
White			
La Roche Pouilly Fuisse	Sonoma County, CA	Chardonnay	$31.29
Simi Sauvignon Blanc	Sonoma County, CA	Sauvignon Blanc	$12.99
Domaine De La Rossignole Sancerre	Verigny, France	Sancerre	$22.39

Chapter 5

The Four Couples Club

The Four Couples Club is probably the most common type of club. The frequent genesis for this club is at a dinner party, where toward the end of the evening someone says, "We should do this more often." The beauty of the structure of this club is in its simplicity: four couples decide they want to get together over dinner on a semiregular basis.

Organization

While my wife and I lived in Delaware, we had a great Four Couples Club. It started as a dinner party that led to an organization meeting where the principles of the club were decided by answering some basic questions:

- Who would be in the club?
- How often do we want to meet?
- How sophisticated do we want this club to be?
- Do we need substitutes?
- What are the host's responsibilities?

- Do we want to delegate the cooking?
- Who will develop the menu?
- How will we divvy up the costs?

With answers to these questions, the rest was easy.

Club Makeup

The smaller the group, the more critical the club makeup becomes. Club members are usually people you know from your neighborhood, work, club and church and parents of your kids' friends. One easy way to broaden your search is to put something out to your Facebook friends. Getting a group of people who like each other and have similar interests can be tough.

We have friends who had what they thought was a great group only to have it blow up over politics. After five years of a successful club, one night over too many glasses of wine, the dinner conversation turned into a heated political debate. The evening ended abruptly (but maybe too late) with one guy storming out of the house. Apologies were made a few days later, but things were never the same.

Substitutes

Given the example above, no matter how close a group seems, it is always good to have substitute members. The primary reason for subs is that despite how well you plan, there are always going to be scheduling conflicts and the need for last minute fill-ins.

A good rule of thumb is that you need to have at least as many subs as you have regular members. Subs also have the potential to become the primary source of future members. It is a great way to introduce couples to the club in a relatively low-stress manner. Many people deal with the "intimidation factor" of having to host a dinner party, and there is no better way to get through that than to have a good experience as a guest.

Scheduling

Many clubs start out trying to meet once a month. The smaller and closer the group is, the more possible meeting once a month is. The key is to always have a future date on the calendar. Too many clubs fall apart as victims of lack of scheduling.

Host Responsibilities

Primary host responsibilities include:
- Scheduling and communicating about the dinner
- Menu development
- Delegation of who prepares (or brings) what
- Setup and execution of the dinner party
- Cost allocation

Menu Development

The host should either develop the menu or delegate this responsibility. One simple way to do so is to use the end of a dinner party to survey the group for ideas.

Some simple questions can be used as a starter:
- Does anyone have an idea for our next supper club?
- What about a theme? Have you been to a restaurant lately where you thought the menu might be good for a supper club dinner?
- Is there something you have been wanting to make?
- Have you seen something on a cooking show that might be interesting to try?

Getting everyone involved in developing the menu is a good idea. That way you get ownership and commitment. The host also needs to be careful to maintain some control. If your discussion happens late at a dinner, sometimes the wine can influence it. You would not want to commit to something too complex or too dangerous. It would be my luck where someone just back from Hawaii wants to dig a pit in my backyard to roast a pig over hot coals.

Menu development can be as hard or as easy as you want to make it. While the Internet is the primary source for most recipes, there is a downside to using untested recipes. I have been part of too many supper clubs where the menu developer pulled something off of the Internet and used it for a club dinner without testing it. A great example of this was a recent club recipe that called for beef tenderloin to be cooked to 140°F. I know from experience that beef cooked to 140°F will be overdone. We are not talking medium well; we are talking shoe leather. I also know the author of the menu and her propensity to "follow" recipes without testing them and that she would be offended by me telling her she didn't know what she was doing. Being ever the diplomat, I sent her and the other hosts using the recipe a note saying, "While some recipes call for 140°F, you might want to target 126°F." The author came back with, "the recipe from the southern league cookbook calls for 140°F." Fortunately, they targeted 126°F. Having written many menus, I have always tried to test dishes out first. I will usually just test a recipe on my family. For larger clubs (and this book), I have had "trial runs" on the menus. Practice makes perfect.

Mise en Place

What is easy for one person can be very difficult for someone else. When a friend (with lesser culinary skills) first saw the piattini menu below, her reaction was "17 pages?!" While the quantity of dishes was a little daunting to her, with some guidance and assistance, she hosted a wonderful party. My first words of advice were to delegate. She had four other couples coming to her party. It was easy to delegate six of the eight menu items. After delegation, the next key is preparation. Most things can be (and should be) done in advance. For example, the meatball recipe below may seem pretty complex at first glance. In reality, the meatballs are best when made a day or two ahead of time, held in the refrigerator until an hour or two before show time, and then heated up in the oven for 20 minutes. The chili sauce for the meatballs is store bought. In the end, I was able to convince my friend that it was pretty easy. Though she did say, "It is easy for YOU."

Costs

There are a couple ways to handle cost:
- Each host covers the cost for their dinner party. (This has a downside in that without a lot of direction what is a "reasonable" cost can come into question.)
- The host keeps track of all costs and divides by four using the model outlined previously:

Cost Example

	Costs	Avg. Cost	Net
Couple 1 (hosts)	$175.00	–$67.00	$108.00
Couple 2	35.00	–67.00	–32.00
Couple 3	15.00	–67.00	–52.00
Couple 4	43.00	–67.00	–24.00
	$268.00	–$268.00	$0.00

Average cost $67.00

Menu Example

Piattini means "small plates" in Italian. The approach to this menu is a little different. Instead of a sit-down dinner, the execution of this menu works best as two or three informal seatings. It is meant to be more like a tasting menu, spread across the course of the evening. The dinner should be a combination of good food with nice wine and great conversation.

The first seating can be served in the kitchen or around a coffee table in a living area. Throughout the meal, the menu items should be served family style on a platter with everyone having their own piattino (small plate). Plating is a little easier with the platters, but you should try to "dress" the platter with herbs or sauce as decoration.

The second seating should be served at a table because the menu items can be messy. (Beets can be dangerous on white rugs…ask Susan, I have the scars to prove it.) Since this seating also has the most menu items, a table seating works best.

Following is a piattini menu that would be great for a four couples club.

Piattini Menu
First Seating
Salami Stuffed with Asparagus and Pesto Cream Cheese
Cheese Puffs with Bacon and Shallot
Second Seating
Roasted Beets with Fresh Mozzarella and Balsamic Reduction
Char-Roasted Garlic Bread with Arugula
Brussels Sprouts with Caramelized Garlic and Bacon
Tomato and Watermelon Salad with Olive Oil and Basil
Mozzarella Stuffed Meatballs with a Sweet Chile Sauce
Dessert
Spiced Chocolate Mousse

salami stuffed with asparagus pesto cream cheese

This recipe can be made ahead of time and stored in the refrigerator for up to 24 hours.

Ingredients

1 8-ounce package Philadelphia cream cheese, softened at room temperature for 2 hours (or cut into 8 pieces and warmed in microwave on high for 1 minute)

6 tablespoons Basil Pesto (see below)

½ pound Boar's Head Genoa salami, sliced thin (but not shaved)

1 pound asparagus (the thinner the better), steamed or blanched until fork-tender

1. Steam asparagus in microwave on high for 4–5 minutes. Set aside to cool.

2. In the bowl of a food processor fitted with a metal blade, combine the softened cream cheese and 6 tablespoons of pesto.

3. Pulse to combine.

4. Work in batches of 3 slices of salami. (Note: it works best if the salami has been tempered at room temperature for 30 minutes.)

5. Spread a tablespoon of cream cheese mixture on the salami.

6. Add the asparagus.

7. Roll it up to form a wrap.

Cookware Needed

Food processor

Serves 8 People

Step	Prep Time
Prep and cool asparagus	10–15 min
Combine ingredients in food processor	1–2 min
Assemble salami rolls	10–15 min
Total	**21-32 min**

Cook Time	Temperature
Steam asparagus in microwave	High for 4-5 min
Total	**4-5 min**

basil pesto

Ingredients

1 cup fresh basil

2 good-sized cloves garlic

½ cup shelled walnuts

½ cup extra virgin olive oil

¾ cup freshly grated Parmesan or Romano cheese

1 pinch red pepper flakes

Salt and pepper to taste

Cookware Needed
Food processor

Serves 8 People

Step	Prep Time
Prep basil, garlic, nuts, etc.	3–5
Combine ingredients in food processor	1–2
Total	4-7 min

1. In the bowl of a food processor fitted with a metal blade, combine basil, garlic and walnuts. Process into a rough paste.

2. With processor running, drizzle in olive oil.

3. Add Parmesan, red pepper flakes, salt and pepper.

4. Gently pulse to combine, being careful not to overwork the pesto.

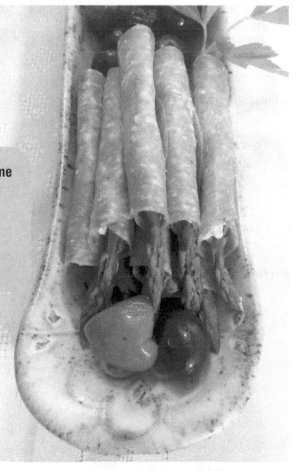

cheese puffs with bacon and shallot

Ingredients

½ pound Oscar Mayer bacon, chopped in ¼-inch dice

1 stick unsalted butter

½ cup shallots, finely minced

1 cup milk

1 cup all purpose flour

5 eggs

2 cups grated Parmesan cheese (blends of Parmesan and Romano or Parmesan and Swiss also work well)

Pam cooking spray

1 teaspoon kosher salt

Cookware Needed

Medium pot

Mini muffin pan

10 or 12 inch sauté (or frying) pans

Serves 8 People

1. Preheat oven to 400°F.

2. Sauté bacon until fully rendered. Drain the fat and set aside.

3. In a medium sized pot, melt the butter.

4. Add shallots and sauté under low heat until the shallots become translucent (4 minutes).

5. Add milk and bring to a boil.

6. Take the pot off of the heat. Add flour and stir vigorously with a wooden spoon until flour and butter are combined.

7. Add four of the eggs, one at a time, stirring each with the wooden spoon until all four are incorporated.

8. Add 1½ cups of Parmesan cheese, ¾ of the bacon and salt. Fold together into the dough.

9. Spray a nonstick mini muffin pan with Pam.

10. Spoon a tablespoon of the dough into each muffin cup.

11. Scramble the remaining egg in a separate bowl. Brush each dough ball with the egg wash.

12. Sprinkle on the remaining Parmesan cheese and bacon as a topping.

13. Place in oven and cook for 25 minutes or until the puffs are a deep golden brown.

14. Remove puffs from the pan and serve.

Note: You can make these an hour in advance. Remove them from the pan and reheat in a 350°F oven for 5 minutes.

Cook Time	Temperature
Sauté bacon	Medium for 7-10 min
Melt butter	Medium for 3-5 min
Sauté shallot	Medium-low for 5-6 min
Add milk and bring to boil	Medium-low for 5-7 min
Add flour and eggs	7-8 min
Add cheese and bacon	3-5 min
Bake cheese puffs	385°F for25–30
Total	**55-71 min**

Step	Prep Time
Assemble ingredients	3–5 min
Fill and prep mini muffin pan	5–10 min
Final prep and presentation	3–5 min
Total	**11-20 min**

mozzarella-stuffed meatballs

Ingredients

¾ cup Italian-style breadcrumbs

¼ cup milk

½ pound chopped sirloin

½ pound sweet Italian sausage, taken out of the casing

½ pound hot Italian sausage

½ pound chopped veal

1½ cups onion, finely chopped

3 tablespoons garlic, finely minced

1 cup Italian parsley

1 cup Parmesan cheese, roughly grated

2 eggs

Kosher salt and pepper to taste

6 sticks of whole fat mozzarella string cheese, cut into ½-inch pieces

1 cup olive oil

Thai sweet chili sauce*

Cookware Needed

10 or 12 inch sauté (or frying) pan (I use two at a time to fry meatballs to expedite the process

Baking sheet

Serves 8-15 People

1. Preheat oven to 375°F.

2. Place the breadcrumbs in a small bowl and stir in milk. Set aside to allow the milk to absorb.

3. In a large mixing bowl, place the chopped sirloin, sausage, veal, onion, garlic, parsley, Parmesan cheese, breadcrumbs, eggs, salt and pepper.

4. Roll up your sleeves, wash your hands, and then go to town mixing all of the ingredients. You want to have all the ingredients well blended.

5. Wet your hands under running water. Place a golf ball-sized spoonful of raw meatball (about 1.5 inches in diameter) in one hand. Push a ½-inch piece of mozzarella into the middle. Roll the meatball in your hand to round it out and cover the cheese with meat.

6. Repeat the process until all the meatballs are formed.

7. Liberally coat the bottom of a large sauté pan with olive oil. Heat under medium-high heat until the oil just begins to smoke. Add the first batch of meatballs. Using tongs, rotate the meatball as each side browns. When the first set of meatballs is browned, place them on a cooking sheet lined with aluminum foil. Note: You just want to brown the meatballs. You don't need them to be cooked through.

8. Repeat the process with subsequent batches. You will have to add oil as you go along.

Step	Prep Time
Soak breadcrumbs in milk	3–4 min
Combine meat and other ingredients	4–8 min
Make meatballs	5–10 min
Total	**12-22 min**

9. When all the meatballs are browned, place them in the oven and cook for 20 minutes until each is cooked through.

10. Serve with: Thai sweet chili sauce (available in most supermarkets)

Note: I made three versions of this sauce with recipes I found online. When I tested them against two store-bought versions, the sweet chili sauce from the local supermarket won hands down. My recommendation is to go with the store bought!

Cook Time	Temperature
Fry meatballs (2 minutes per side × 3)	Medium-high for 15–20
Bake meatballs to finish	375°F for 20–25
Total	**55-71 min**

roasted beets with fresh mozzarella and balsamic reduction

Ingredients

3 good-sized beets, washed and the stems removed

¼ cup extra virgin olive oil

Salt and freshly ground pepper to taste

6 ounces fresh mozzarella sliced (the buffalo mozzarella in water at Costco is outstanding)

Balsamic Reduction (see below)

2 tablespoons chiffonade-cut basil leaves

Cookware Needed

Aluminum foil

Baking sheet

Serves 8 People

1. Preheat oven to 380°F.

2. Cut beets in half. Brush with olive oil and sprinkle generously with salt and pepper.

3. Place the beets flat side down on a large sheet of aluminum foil. Wrap into a packet and place on a baking sheet.

4. Bake for 50 minutes or until the beets are fork-tender.

5. After beets have cooled, peel off the outer skin (optional; I personally prefer to capture the char note on the skin).

6. Cut into 1-inch pieces and mix in a bowl with 4 tablespoons of olive oil, salt and pepper.

7. Place the beets on a plate next to slice of fresh mozzarella.

8. Drizzle the plate with the balsamic reduction.

9. Top with basil and a grind of fresh pepper.

Step	Prep Time
Prep beets	3–5 min
Prep mozzarella, basil, etc.	2–3 min
Final prep and presentation	3–5 min
Total	**12-22 min**

Cook Time	Temperature
Bake beets	380°F for 50–60 min
Total	**50-60 min**

balsamic reduction

Ingredients

3 good-sized beets, washed ¾ cup balsamic vinegar

2 tablespoons maple syrup

1 heaping teaspoon cornstarch

Cookware Needed

Medium saucepan

Wire whisk

Serves 8 People

1. Heat balsamic vinegar in a saucepan, bringing to a boil and reducing by 25%.

2. Add maple syrup and bring to a boil.

3. Thicken with a teaspoon of cornstarch diluted in a ¼ cup of cold water.

4. Whisk.

Cook Time	Temperature
Reduce balsamic	High for 8-10 min
Add honey and cornstarch/thicken	High for 5-10 min
Total	**13-20 min**

Step	Prep Time
General prep	3–5
Total	**3-5 min**

tomato and watermelon salad with olive oil and basil

Ingredients

1 10-ounce package grape tomatoes

3½ cups seedless watermelon, cut into 1-inch chunks

15 Kalamata olives, cut in halves lengthwise

2 tablespoons capers

¼ cup olive oil

Kosher salt and fresh ground pepper

¼ cup Italian basil, coarsely chopped

Cookware Needed

Mixing bowl

Serves 8 People

1. Cut grape tomatoes into halves and add to a mixing bowl.

2. Add watermelon, olives and capers.

3. Drizzle in the olive oil while mixing.

4. Season aggressively with salt and pepper.

5. Sprinkle with basil and serve.

Step	Prep Time
Prep watermelon	3–5
Prep tomatoes, olives and capers	3–4
Final prep and presentation	3–4
Total	**12-22 min**

brussels sprouts with bacon and caramelized garlic with mustard dill sauce

Ingredients

16 good-sized Brussels sprouts

6 strips thick-cut bacon, cut into ¼-inch pieces

12 cloves garlic, cut into thin slices

¾ cup onion, roughly diced

3 tablespoons flour

2+ cups canola oil for frying

Mustard Dill Sauce (see right)

Cookware Needed

10 or 12 inch sauté (or frying) pan

Large frying pan

Baking sheet

Serves 8 People

Step	Prep Time
Prep Brussels sprouts	10–15
Total	10-15 min

1. Take the leaves off of the Brussels sprouts. This process is a little funky. The goal is to get as many leaves as possible. I use a paring knife and keep cutting into the core of the Brussels sprout and pulling off leaves. There comes a point where you are left with a core, and that's OK. Throw the small core into your pile of leaves for frying.

2. In a sauté pan, brown the bacon. Set aside.

3. In the same pan, drain off the most of the bacon fat, leaving a tablespoon or two. Add garlic and onion. Sauté on medium heat until nicely caramelized.

4. Add the bacon, mix, then set aside off of the heat.

5. Put Brussels sprout leaves into a large plastic bag. Add flour and shake to roughly coat.

6. In a large frying pan, heat the canola oil until it almost smokes.

7. Separate Brussels sprout leaves into two batches. Fry each batch separately until the leaves begin to brown. Take them out of the frying pan and set them on a paper towel to drain off the excess oil.

8. When both batches of Brussels sprouts leaves have been fried and drained, place them on a cooking sheet lined with aluminum foil, and set in the oven at 200°F to be kept warm.

9. Just before serving, combine Brussels sprout leaves with the garlic/onion/bacon mixture.

Cook Time	Temperature
Sauté bacon	Medium for 7-10 min
Sauté garlic and onion	Medium-low for 7-10 min
Fry Brussels sprouts leaves	Medium-high for 7-10 min
Warm Brussels sprouts in oven	200°F for 10-15 min
Total	**30-43 min**

mustard dill sauce

Ingredients

3 tablespoons Dijon mustard

3 teaspoons white sugar

¼ teaspoon white pepper

2 tablespoons chopped fresh dill

2 tablespoons white wine vinegar

½ cup olive oil

1 heaping teaspoon dry mustard powder

Salt and pepper to taste

Cookware Needed

Food processor

Serves 8 People

1. Combine all the ingredients in the bowl of a food processor fitted with a metal blade.

2. Process until it achieves the thickness of a thin mayonnaise.

3. Put into a covered bowl and refrigerate for at least 2 hours.

Note: Sauce can be made 2 days in advance.

Step	Prep Time
Combine ingredients in food processor	1–2
Cool in refrigerator	120–130
Total	**121-132 min**

char roasted garlic bread

Ingredients

15 whole cloves garlic, peeled

4 tablespoons olive oil

1 teaspoon kosher salt

1 stick unsalted butter,
softened to room temperature

2 tablespoons Italian parsley

1 French baguette,
cut in half lengthwise
(the baguette at Costco
is best for this as it
fairly dense and crusty)

1 bunch arugula,
roughly chopped
(if arugula is hard to find,
it can be replaced with
½ cup Italian parsley
and ½ cup fresh dill)

Cookware Needed

Baking sheet

Aluminum foil

Serves 8 People

1. Preheat oven to 400°F.

2. Place garlic cloves on a sheet of aluminum foil.

3. Brush with 2 tablespoons olive oil and sprinkle with salt.

4. Fold the foil into a packet and roast in oven for 15 minutes or until garlic turns slightly brown. Let cool.

5. In a food processor fitted with a metal blade, combine softened butter, roasted garlic, salt and parsley.

6. Pulse into a paste. (Note: You might want to make extra of this compound butter because it can make shoe leather taste good. Use it for grilled steak, seafood, and vegetables. It is great for a quick pasta dish. You can keep it in the refrigerator for a few weeks and in the freezer for months.)

7. Spread the butter liberally onto the open side of the baguette halves.

8. Place the baguette halves butter side-down on a cookie sheet lined with aluminum foil.

9. Bake at 390°F for 30 minutes or until the butter chars slightly into a dark brown crust.

10. Toss the arugula with one tablespoon of olive oil.

11. Cut the bread into 1-inch slices.

12. Top with arugula and serve.

Step	Prep Time
Prep garlic	3–5 min
Combine ingredients in food processor	1–2 min
Slice and butter bread	1–2 min
Toss arugula with olive oil and top bread	3–5 min
Total	**10-15 min**

Cook Time	Temperature
Roast garlic	400°F for 15–18 min
Bake garlic bread	390°F for 30–35 min
Total	**45-53 min**

spiced chocolate mousse

Ingredients

12 ounces bittersweet or semisweet chocolate

1 teaspoon chili powder

5 tablespoons honey

2½ cups chilled heavy whipping cream

1 small package fresh raspberries

1 tablespoon confectioner's sugar

Cookware Needed

Small saucepan

Mixing bowl

Serves 8 People

1. In a medium saucepan, stir chocolate, chili powder, honey and ¾ cup of cream over a low heat until the chocolate melts and mixture is smooth. Cool, stirring occasionally.

2. In a large bowl, beat 1¼ cups of cream until soft peaks form. Fold cream into the chocolate mixture in two additions. Divide mouse among 8 ramekins.

3. Refrigerate until set, about 2 hours.

4. Whip remaining cream and confectioner's sugar to firm peaks. Spoon one dollop of cream on the center of each ramekin and top with a few raspberries.

Step	Prep Time
Whip cream	5–10 min
Fold whipped cream into chocolate	2–3 min
Refrigerate mousse	120 min
Final prep and presentation	5–10 min
Total	**132–143 min**

Cook Time	Temperature
Cook chocolate/cream mixture	Low for 5–10 min
Total	45-53 min

Prep Schedule—Mise en Place (for a Saturday evening dinner)
Thursday
Make Lobster stock
Fry meatballs
Friday
Make stuffed salami
Make mousse
Roast beets
Make balsamic reduction
Saturday
5:20 PM   Prep crudités
10:00 AM Prep Brussels sprouts, bacon and onion
1:00 PM   Make cheese puffs
4:00   Prep garlic bread butter
5:00   Make tomato/watermelon salad
5:10   Fry Brussels sprouts
6:00   Plate beets, mozzarella and balsamic
6:30   Bake meatballs and garlic bread
6:45   Warm cheese puffs and Brussels sprouts
7:10   Guests arrive, serve wine
7:15   Chit chat
7:30   Assemble and serve cheese puffs and salami
7:50   Finish and serve meatballs, beets, bread and sprouts
9:00   Finish and serve dessert

Wine Recommendations

Wine	Origin	Composition	Price
Red			
Liberty School Cabernet	Paso Robles, CA	Cabernet Sauvignon	$16.00
Susan Balbo Malbec	Mendoza, Argentina	Malbec	$27.99
Belle Glos Pinot Noir	Santa Barbara,CA	Pinot Noir	$39.00
White			
Matchbook Chardonnay	Zamora, CA	Chardonnay	$15.00
Chateau Ste. Michelle	Horsehead Vineyard, WA	Sauvignon Blanc	$15.99
Loredona Viognier	California	Viognier	$7.50

Chapter 6

Send Out an Email

This form of supper club is my daughter's creation. Jenn loves to entertain (something about apples and trees...). She also has a built-in social network with her husband's work associates. As new parents, they particularly like dining at home, where they can put their and their friend's babies down to sleep. The process starts with Jenn sending out an email telling friends that they are hosting a party. The email would specify:

- Date (a few days to a few weeks out).
- Theme.
- What the host is making.
- Ideas for sides and dessert and ask for volunteers to bring those items.

Organization

The organization of this type of club is pretty loose. It also evolves with the makeup of the group. The host must let participants know the date and theme of the dinner. The organization evolves around the responses the host gets from that initial email.

Club Makeup

The makeup of the group can be as large as your email contact list or as small as your next-door neighbors. The informality of this type of club can be a good basis for more for structured groups that can evolve.

Scheduling

Scheduling is at the whim of the initiator. The general rule is a couple of weeks out, but sometimes the more spontaneous a dinner party is, the more fun it is. This type of supper club tends to get scheduled randomly. It may be a few months between dinner parties, but it can also be a few weeks.

Substitutes

It is always good to have potential substitutes, though with this group, it might get dicey. It could be embarrassing to call someone at the last minute saying, "Hey, we are having a dinner party that everyone else has known about for weeks and were wondering if you are interested in coming at the last minute." Discretion is always good. You just need a few flexible friends. Like with everything else, it usually isn't what you say, but how you say it. It is good to have a few friends that you can call at the last minute. If the food, company and wine are good, people are just glad to be invited.

Host Responsibilities

The hosts really take the lead with this group. They should:
- Set the date.
- Decide on a theme.
- Establish a basic outline of the menu.
- Send out the email or series of emails.
- Coordinate the appetizers, side dishes, etc. and/or other responsibilities.
- Prepare the main course.

Other Responsibilities

The informality and spontaneity of this type of group also lends itself to delegating responsibilities. For example, the host can designate people to:

- Bring choice beverages.
- Bring dinnerware.
- Set up.
- Clean up.
- Figure out entertainment.
- Do anything else the host needs help with.

Menu Development

Generally, there is not a formal menu developed in advance. The host should ask participants to respond if they can attend and what they would like to bring. The host keeps track of responses and must manage the menu a bit to make sure, for example, four people bring don't bring Mexican dips.

Have you ever wondered why some people bring shrimp cocktail to every event? You know, the ones you buy in the supermarket with watery precooked shrimp and jarred cocktail sauce. I love shrimp as much as the next guy, but there is little as bland as these puppies. One of my favorite old lines is "Nothing influences the flavor of food more than how it is cooked." It isn't "Nothing influences the flavor of food more than how it is defrosted." Though it is true that one of our goals is to keep menu items simple and easy, there has to be some discretion.

Mise en Place

Things that can be made in advance and just warmed in the oven work really well for this type of club. As a rule, if you have to cook something to temperature, the process and chance of success gets a little more complicated and risky.

I often get asked something like "How long do you grill that for?" There just isn't a good answer, since multiple factors impact the doneness of a piece of meat:

- How hot the grill is

- If the grill is gas or charcoal
- The thickness of meat
- If the heat is direct or indirect
- How many times you lift the grill lid

After I go through this explanation, I invariably get asked, "Can you teach my husband to grill? He always overcooks everything." And yes, some people like overcooked meat, but they are becoming more and more the minority (chefs that I know at high end restaurants say 75% of customers prefer medium rare).

At Kraft Food Ingredients, we tried to train our salespeople to cook meat to temperature. It isn't easy at first, but with practice and a little technique, anyone can get pretty good. What we did for training was to cook three pieces of meat, one rare, one medium and one well done, and asked people to touch them for firmness. The rare one is soft. The well done was hard. The medium was in between the hard and soft. This is what real chefs do, and it works.

One of the best chefs I ever worked with would use the touch test to get a piece of meat past rare and then use a knife to make a quick check to confirm. This breaks the rule that you don't want to pierce the meat to preserve the juices. If the combination of the touch test and a small slice works for great chefs, it works for me. Besides, that one piece you cut and throw back on the grill can be served to the guy who likes his meat well done. He won't know the difference anyway.

I was once cooking for a guy that was a real germophobe. He saw me touch his steak for doneness and said, "I am not going to eat that…you touched it." I told him that every steak he has ever had at a restaurant had been "touched" by the chef for doneness. If he had a problem with someone touching his food, he would starve at my house.

Costs

The informal nature of this type of club lends itself to each couple paying for what they bring. If costs become an issue, you can always fall back on the cost allocation model outlined in previous chapters.

Send an Email Italian Menu
Antipasto
Salami, Provolone, Olives, White Beans
Main Course
Lasagna
Sides
Grill Roasted Italian Sausages
Chopped Salad with Italian Dressing
Garlic Bread
Grilled Eggplant with Tomato Concassé
Dessert
Cannoli

antipasto

Ingredients

½ pound Genoa salami,
sliced thin

¼ pound chunk of
sharp provolone,
cut into ¼-inch thick slices

1 8-ounce container
mixed olives

1 4-ounce container
white beans

Serves 8 People

Step	Prep Time
Arrange on a platter	3–5 min
Total	**3-5 min**

Arrange on a plate and serve.

Note: All of the ingredients can be purchased at a decent supermarket deli/olive bar

quick tomato sauce

Ingredients

10 cloves garlic, peeled and sliced thin

1 medium onion, diced

¼ cup extra virgin olive oil

1 large can (28 ounces) whole tomatoes

2 small cans (6 ounces each) tomato paste

1 tablespoon dried oregano

1 tablespoon dried thyme

2 teaspoons black pepper

2 teaspoons kosher salt

2 teaspoons sugar

¼ teaspoon red pepper flakes

Cookware Needed

Large pot

10 or 12 inch sauté (or frying) pan

Serves 8 People

1. In a large pan, sauté garlic and onion in olive oil over a low heat until translucent, being careful not to burn the garlic.

2. Add can of whole tomatoes, crushing the tomatoes by hand as you add.

3. In the empty can, put one small can of tomato paste and fill ¾ with water. Whisk until water is dispersed.

4. Repeat the above with the second can then add both to the pot.

5. Add the remaining ingredients.

6. Bring to a simmer and cover.

7. Simmer for 30–40 minutes (can be used immediately as it doesn't need to cool).

Step	Prep Time
Prep garlic and onion	5–8 min
Combine in large pot	1–2 min
Total	**6-10 min**

Cook Time	Temperature
Sauté garlic and onion	Medium-low for 5–7 min
Simmer sauce	Medium-low for 30–40 min
Total	**35–47 min**

Tancredi albanevoli's lasagna

Ingredients

1 eggplant, sliced into ⅜-inch slices

1 cup flour

1 teaspoon salt

1 teaspoon pepper

1 cup olive oil

1 pound Italian sausage, taken out of casing

1 large container (30 ounces) whole milk ricotta cheese

1 cup Parmesan cheese, grated

2 eggs

1 cup Italian parsley, chopped

1 pot Quick Tomato Paste (see below)

1 12-ounce box oven-ready lasagna noodles (the quick-cooking kind)

3 cups low-moisture mozzarella cheese, grated

1 disposable aluminum lasagna pan, 13½ × 9⅝ × 2¾.

Cookware Needed

Two 10 or 12 inch sauté (or frying) pan

1 disposable aluminum lasagna pan, 13½ × 9⅝ × 2¾.

Serves 8 People

1. Preheat oven to 375°F.

2. Dredge the eggplant slices in flour seasoned with salt and pepper.

3. In a large sauté pan, heat ¼ cup olive oil. Sauté eggplant slices in batches (2 or 3 at a time) until slightly golden. Place fried slices on a paper towel to drain.

4. In another large sauté pan, brown sausage, using a wooden spatula to break it into small pieces.

5. In a large mixing bowl, gently mix ricotta cheese, Parmesan cheese, eggs and parsley.

6. Ladle tomato sauce into the lasagna pan, adding enough to coat the bottom.

7. Add a layer of lasagna noodles.

8. Add a layer of half of the ricotta mixture.

9. Add a layer of browned sausage.

10. Add a layer of tomato sauce.

11. Add a layer of lasagna noodles.

12. Add a layer of the remaining ricotta mixture.

13. Add a layer of eggplant slices.

14. Add a layer of tomato sauce.

15. Add a layer of lasagna noodles.

16. Add a layer of tomato sauce.

17. Top with a layer of mozzarella.

18. Cover roasting pan with aluminum foil and bake for 45 minutes.

Cook Time	Temperature
Sauté eggplant (per side)	Medium for 3–5 min
Brown sausage	Medium-high for 6–8 min
Bake lasagna (covered with foil)	375°F for 45–50 min
Bake lasagna (uncovered)	375°F for 10–15 min
Total	**64–78 min**

Step	Prep Time
Prep eggplant	3–5 min
Mix ricotta, Parmesan and egg	3–5 min
Assemble lasagna	5–10 min
Let baked lasagna rest	15–20 min
Total	**3-5 min**

19. Remove aluminum foil and bake for another 15 minutes or until cheese is golden brown.

20. Remove from oven and let lasagna temper at room temperature for 15 minutes.

Note: The lasagna can be made in advance warmed up at the last minute. The best procedure for reheating is to remove the pan from the refrigerator for 1 hour to slack out. Cover with aluminum foil and place in a 375°F oven for 20 minutes. Uncover and cook for another 10 minutes. Remove from oven and let lasagna temper at room temp for 15 minutes before serving.

grill-roasted italian sausages

Sometimes the things that challenge a layman are a simple solution for a real chef. For years, I struggled to grill sausages. Invariably, the heat of the grill would cause flare-ups with the fat in the sausages and result in burned exteriors and uncooked interiors. One day, I complained about this dilemma to chef Lucien Vendome. Lucien gave me a "I thought you were smarter than that" look and said, "The solution is easy: mark the sausages on the grill, infusing them with the 'grill flavor,' and then finish them in the oven."

Ingredients
1 pound sweet Italian sausages
1 pound hot Italian sausages

Cookware Needed
Gas grill
Baking sheet

Serves 8 People

1. Preheat your grill to get it very hot. Preheat oven to 400°F.

2. Grill the sausages until they are well marked but not burned.

3. Place them on a cooking sheet and finish cooking in oven for 10 minutes or until they are cooked through.

Step	Prep Time
Preheat grill	5–10 min
Total	**5-10 min**

Cook Time	Temperature
Grill sausages until marked	Medium-high for 5–10 min
Bake sausages in oven	400°F for 10–12 min
Total	**15-22 min**

roasted garlic bread with italian parsley

Ingredients

1 head garlic (10 or so cloves), peeled and roughly chopped

1 medium shallot, peeled and roughly chopped

1 stick unsalted butter, tempered for an hour at room temperature

1 teaspoon kosher salt

½ teaspoon black pepper

¼ cup olive oil

1 cup Italian parsley, coarsely chopped

1 French baguette (the denser and crustier the bread, the better)

Cookware Needed

Baking sheet

Aluminum foil

Food processor

Serves 8 People

Step	Prep Time
Prep garlic	3–5
Combine ingredients in food processor	1–2
Slice and butter bread	1–2
Sprinkle bread with parsley	3–5
Total	8-14 min

1. Preheat oven to 380°F.

2. Sauté garlic and shallot in olive oil under low heat for 10 minutes or until the garlic and shallot become translucent. Be sure to use a low heat to reduce the risk of scorching the garlic, as burnt garlic has bitter side notes. Set aside to cool.

3. Place the softened butter into a food processor fitted with a metal blade. Add the garlic, shallot, salt and pepper. Pulse to incorporate. Do not overblend.

4. Cut the baguette in half lengthwise.

5. Place two pieces of baguette face up on a cooking sheet lined with aluminum foil.

6. Roast the bread in oven for 15 minutes or until the open side of the bread becomes golden brown.

7. Remove from oven and spread a liberal amount of compound butter on the bread.

8. At the end, sprinkle on the chopped parsley and serve.

Cook Time	Temperature
Sauté garlic	Medium-low for 3–5 min
Bake garlic bread	380°F for 15–20 min
Total	18-24 min

chopped salad with italian dressing

Ingredients

1 medium-sized head romaine lettuce, chopped into ½-inch slices

¼ cup red onion, sliced thin

¼ pound Genoa salami, sliced thin and then cut into ¼-inch julienned slices

1 cup low-moisture mozzarella cheese, grated

1 cup grape tomatoes, cut into halves

1 cup Kalamata olives, cut into halves

2 hard-boiled eggs, coarsely chopped

½ cup hearts of palm, roughly chopped

Italian Dressing (see below)

Cookware Needed

Mixing bowl

Serves 8 People

1. In a large salad bowl, toss all ingredients except the dressing.

2. Add ½ cup of Italian Dressing and toss lightly. Taste to assess if there is enough dressing. Add more as needed.

Step	Prep Time
Prep lettuce, salami, onion, etc.	5–8
Grate cheese	3–4
Total	**8-12min**

italian dressing

Ingredients

2 cloves garlic, finely chopped/mashed with ½ teaspoon kosher salt

¼ cup red wine vinegar

1 teaspoon Dijon mustard

½ cup extra virgin olive oil

1 teaspoon dried oregano

½ teaspoon black pepper

Cookware Needed

Mixing bowl

Serves 8 People

1. In a medium bowl, add the mashed garlic, vinegar and mustard. Whisk to blend.

2. Add the olive oil in a drizzle, whisking vigorously to emulsify.

3. Whisk in the oregano and the pepper then set aside..

Step	Prep Time
Prep garlic	3–5
Whisk to combine ingredients	3–4
Total	**6-9 min**

grilled eggplant with tomato concassé

Ingredients

1 medium eggplant

¼ cup red wine vinegar

¼ cup olive oil

Salt and pepper

Cookware Needed

Gas grill

Serves 8 People

1. Preheat a gas grill to high temperature.

2. Cut the eggplant lengthwise into ⅜-inch slices

3. Brush olive oil on both sides and liberally sprinkle with salt and pepper.

4. Grill eggplant for about 3 minutes on each side so that grill marks are pronounced but eggplant is not overcooked.

5 As you pull slices off the grill, brush with vinegar.

6. Place eggplant slices on a serving platter and add a spoonful of the tomato concassé to each slice.

7. Serve.

Step	Prep Time
Prep eggplant	3–5 min
Brush eggplant with vinegar	1–2 min
Total	**3-5 min**

Cook Time	Temperature
Grill eggplant (per side)	High for 3-4 min
Total	6-8 min

tomato concassé

Ingredients

3 plum tomatoes

2 tablespoons extra virgin olive oil

¼ cup red wine vinegar

Salt and pepper to taste

4 green onions, diced into ¼-inch slices (green and white parts)

1 medium shallot, finely diced

3 tablespoons fresh Italian parsley, chopped

Cookware Needed

Mixing bowl

Serves 8 People

1. Cut plum tomatoes lengthwise into 4 quarters. Scrape out the seeds and pulp. Then cut the cored tomato first into ⅜-inch strips and then into ⅜-inch cubes.

2. Place tomato into a medium bowl. Add olive oil and toss lightly.

3. Add vinegar, salt and pepper.

4. Add onion, shallot and parsley to tomato mixture and toss to incorporate.

Step	Prep Time
Prep tomatoes, onion, shallot and parsley	3–5
Mix all ingredients	1–3
Total	**4-8 min**

cannoli

Purchase your favorite kind from your local bakery.

Step	Prep Time
Arrange cannoli on platter	2–3
Total	**2-3 min**

Prep Schedule—Mise en Place (for a Saturday evening dinner)
Friday
Make lasagna
Saturday
10:00 AM	Buy cannoli
2:00 PM	Prep antipasto
4:00	Prep garlic bread butter
4:10	Prep tomato concassé
5:00	Make chopped salad
5:10	Prep and grill sausages
6:00	Grill eggplant
6:30	Bake and warm sausages and garlic bread
6:45	Warm lasagna
7:10	Guests arrive, serve wine
7:15	Chit chat
7:30	Assemble and serve antipasto
7:40	Assemble garlic bread and salad
7:50	Finish and serve lasagna, sausage and eggplant
9:00	Finish and serve dessert

Wine Recommendations

Wine	Origin	Composition	Price
Red			
Sequoia Grove Cabernet	Napa, CA	Cabernet Sauvignon	$38.00
Abstract—Orin Swift	CA	Red Blend	$33.99
Walter Scott La Combe Verte	Willamette Valley, OR	Pinot Noir	$29.00
White			
Kendall Jackson Chardonnay	CA	Chardonnay	$17.99
Cakebread Cellars Sauvignon Blance	Napa Valley, CA	Sauvignon Blanc	$29.99
Fess Parker Viognier	Santa Barbara, CA	Viognier	$19.99

Chapter 7

"I Don't Cook, but I Know Where to Buy"

There are all kinds of supper clubs. The basic premise of this book is that people like to socialize over a meal. This type of club is for people who either don't like to cook, can't cook, don't have the time or are simply not good cooks. In today's "foodie" world, there are all kinds of options to bring people together over a great meal without cooking.

This club is patterned after my daughter's mother-in-law. Helene is a foodie and a great hostess, but she doesn't cook. She and her husband, Rick, bring together great meals by shopping from local markets and restaurants. One of the best things about this type of club is the research. Think of all the fun you can have trying different foods from all kinds of markets and restaurants with the objective of hosting a supper club meal.

Helene and Rick spend their summers in Montauk, New York. Montauk is a fantastic place in the summer. From a year-round population of 3,000, it explodes to over 30,000 during the summer. Located on the very tip of Long Island, it is a 2-hour car or train ride from NYC. Weekends in the summer can get a little crazy as people escape from the city to the seashore.

While there are some great restaurants in Montauk, getting reservations and fighting crowds can be quite a challenge. The perfect answer is a supper club.

It can be tough to get into the your preferred restaurants on a weekend no matter where you are, whether you are in Montauk or have a lake house in Iuka, Mississippi, or live in the city. You can, however, get amazing food from just about any restaurant via takeout.

Club Makeup

This type of club is based on who is out for the weekend or who you see at the beach or run into at Starbucks. Emails and last-minute texts are great to find out who is around on a weekend. One thing about having a place in the Hamptons is that you have a lot of visitors. Every weekend, you can count on family and friends to be around. Without fail, they are hungry for a great meal. Come to think of it, whether you are at a beach house or just hanging out at home, an impromptu dinner party where you don't have to cook is a winner.

Scheduling

This type of club is more of a planned impromptu style. It is certainly more flexible than other types of clubs. A little planning goes a long way to spread the hosting responsibilities around. Having the club evolve to where you have a schedule of hosting responsibilities is ideal. One of the keys is flexibility, as you usually don't know about last-minute additions.

Host Responsibilities

Coming up with the theme and the menu is the first thing the host has to do. For example, when I am out in the Hamptons, my favorite theme is seafood and local produce. It's funny, but when you say "New York" to non–New Yorkers, they think "city." They don't think farms and great local produce. The truth is that during the summer and fall, there are all kinds of farm stands and wonderful local produce. And, the seafood is just phenomenal. Lobster, clams, swordfish, scallops, blue fish, flounder… It is all good!

Coordination and communication are the keys to this type of club. By default, the host has to take over the bulk of this responsibility. The host has to let people know:

- Where
- When
- The theme and menu
- What to bring
- Who is responsible for what

As with the majority of supper clubs, the host does the lion's share of the cleaning. With this type of club (and others) you can delegate the cleaning or even bringing plates and glasses. You may know, for example, that Harry never cooks and his wife really hates hosting. Put him in charge of cleanup. One thing I have seen over the years is that resentment builds up when a couple never wants to host a party. Everyone has a friend like this. You like their company and want to include them, but you know they will never reciprocate. Here is your chance: give that person or persons other jobs.

Mise en Place

The preparation for this type of club is different. It is more about scheduling and coordinating pickup. Helene and Rick out at Montauk will serve a first course and Rick will disappear and run down to Gosman's to pick up the lobster. A 15-minute run to a restaurant to pick up hot food is not that big a deal. With conversation, alcohol and hors d'oeuvres, chances are no one will miss a person or two. Again, with coordination and communication you can be prepared without doing the cooking.

Costs

There are two basic approaches to costs:

1. Pay for what you are asked to bring

2. Total all cost and divide it equally as demonstrated in the classic club formula

Menu Development

This menu is a little different in that not only do you need to think of the items, but you also have to think about where to buy it (again: research is key and, fun).

The following are examples of menus developed for no-cook supper clubs hosted in the Hamptons and Memphis.

Example of coordinating who buys what where

Menu Items	Where	Who
Appetizers		
Seafood Spread	Gosman's Market	Rick
Shallot and Blue Cheese Dip	Citarella's	Bret
Crackers, Crudité and Chips	Citarella's	Bret
Main Course		
Lobsters	Gosman's Market	Rick
Broccoli Cole Slaw	Harvest	Jenn
Potato Salad	Harvest	Jenn
Bread and Butter	Waldbaum's	Susan
French Lentil with Vinaigrette	Citarella's	Bret
Dessert		
Apple Pie	Olish's Farmstand	Billy
Berry Pie	Olish's Farmstand	Billy
Ice Cream	Waldbaum's	Susan
Drinks		
Maker's Mark	BottleHampton	Steve
Wolffer Estate Rosé	BottleHampton	Steve
Kim Crawford Sauvignon Blanc	BottleHampton	Steve
Caldwell Brion Rocket Science	BottleHampton	Steve

Memphis Menu

The beauty of this kind of supper club is you get to enjoy the best local food wherever you are from the comforts of your own home. Living in Memphis and planning an "I Don't Cook, but I Know Where to Buy" dinner, I pretty much need to have a BBQ menu. If you go anywhere in the world tell someone you are from Memphis, the first thing they say is "Elvis." The second thing they say is "BBQ." Memphis BBQ is a great way to feed an impromptu no-cook supper club party.

On my very first night in Memphis, I went to Corky's BBQ and ordered ribs. The waitress asked me if I wanted my ribs "wet or dry." I said, "Excuse me?" and she said, "Y'all a Yankee, you will like your ribs wet." She was right. Memphians are partial to their ribs cooked dry, which means rubbed in a dry spice blend. Yankees like their ribs wet, or cooked with BBQ sauce.

In 1983 I moved from Bedford, New York, to California. At the same time my buddy Jeff Boyd moved from Greenwich, Connecticut, to Australia. Ten years later, we were talking about the cultural difference between Memphis and Melbourne. In midsentence Jeff stops and says, "In both places they call us Yankees. Big difference, in Melbourne it isn't an insult. Says a lot about cultural differences." One thing for sure, us Yankees like wet ribs.

Being from New York and moving to Memphis 25 years ago, I didn't know anything about BBQ. Where I came from, anything you cooked on the grill was BBQ. In Memphis, BBQ means slowed cooked/smoked pork. The big BBQ event in Memphis is the Memphis in May BBQ festival. The event seems to become larger and larger each year. BBQ teams from around the world compete for various prizes. While there is a lot of competition, there is also a lot of drinking. By most accounts, it is just a huge party with a fair amount of BBQ thrown in. During my first year in Memphis, I went to the BBQ festival. Kraft had sponsored a team and had a stand set up for employees. I worked my way up the line to get served and the server asked me in a very southern accent, "Do you want your Q chopped or pulled?" I said, "Excuse me?" The server said again, "Do you want your Q chopped or pulled?" I had no clue what he was talking about, so before asking again, I just mimicked, "Chopped." I now know that after slow cooking the pork in smokers, the cook lets the pork cool and then "pulls" the pork off of the bone. Hence you can get your BBQ pulled. Some people like their Q pulled and then chopped.

The following menu works well in Memphis for an "I Don't Cook, but I Know Where to Buy" impromptu supper club. No matter where you live, there is probably a local specialty that works equally as well. In New York and Chicago, pizza could be a cornerstone. When we lived in Delaware, I could build a menu around blue claw crabs. When we lived in the San Francisco Bay area, it seemed that we built menus around Chardonnay.

Example of coordinating who buys what where

Menu Items	Where	Who
Appetizers		
Spinach and Artichoke Parmesan Dip	Costco	Amy C.
Chips	Costco	Amy C.
Teriyaki Pineapple Meatballs	Costco	Amy C.
Main Course		
BBQ and Ribs	Corky's	Kathy B.
Beans	Corky's	Kathy B.
Slaw	Corky's	Kathy B.
Rolls	Corky's	Kathy B.
Dessert		
Cookies	Fresh Market	Phil R.
Cupcakes	Fresh Market	Phil R.
Ice Cream	Fresh Market	Phil R.
Wine and Drinks		
Prisoner Blend	Germantown Baptist Wine	Scott F
Ruffino Modus Toscana	Germantown Baptist Wine	Scott F
Butterfly Kiss Pinot Grigio	Germantown Baptist Wine	Scott F
Pellegrino	Costco	Amy C.
Other Stuff		
Cocktail Plates	Costco	Joe C.
Dinner Napkins	Costco	Joe C.
Cleanup	N/A	Len L

I Don't Cook, but I Know Where to Buy: Memphis Menu

Appetizers
Spinach and Artichoke Parmesan Dip (Costco)

Chips (Costco)

Teriyaki Pineapple Meatballs (Costco)

Main Course

BBQ and Ribs (Corky's)

Beans (Corky's)

Slaw (Corky's)

Rolls (Corky's)

Dessert
Cookies (Fresh Market)

Cupcakes (Fresh Market)

Ice Cream (Fresh Market)

Drinks
Prisoner Blend (Germantown Baptist Wine & Liquor)

Ruffino Modus Toscana (Germantown Baptist Wine & Liquor)

Butterfly Kiss Pinot Grigio (Germantown Baptist Wine & Liquor)

Pellegrino (Costco)

Chapter 8

The Kickoff Party

With just about every type of supper club, it is a good idea to have a kickoff party. Whether you want to lay out the ground rules for a formal club or just want to get a smaller informal group started, you have to start somewhere. A great theme for a kickoff party is grilled pizza.

Host Responsibilities

The primary responsibilities include menu development, communication and coordination. We have used grilled pizza as a theme a few times. It works really well from a make in advance and final prep standpoint in that with my approach, you precook the pizza on the grill then finish it in a very hot oven just before serving. Each couple brings a pizza, which can be finished in the host's oven.

From an intimidation standpoint, making your own dough really scares people. Like many things, when you know what you are doing it is really easy. When you don't, it is intimidating. I have used two approaches to fix this. As the host, I have made the dough for everyone and provided raw dough for all. I have also worked with a local pizzeria that would sell everyone raw dough. Either way works great. The food processor method works really well to make the dough. The key is using exact measurements and following instructions closely.

Menu Development

Gourmet pizza has been popular for long time. Google it and you will get enough ideas to fill out any menu. I have a tendency to go with a few basics (Margherita and sausage) and then get adventurous from there. The good thing about this type of menu is that the author/host can outline a few parameters and the other cooks can get creative as well.

Mise en Place

Again, the beauty of grilled pizza is that 90% of the work is done in advance. I have had 10 premade pizzas ready in advance and then recooked them in a hot oven. I really believe that pizza is one those foods (like French fries) that are better when cooked more than once.

Costs

Many club formats include an up-front fee. Each couple can kick in $10. Between that and each couple bringing a pizza and BYOB, costs should not be a challenge for a kickoff party.

Menu Example

Pizza has become one of my specialties of the house. It has gotten to the point that if Susan and I entertain, guests expect my grilled pizzas. To be honest, I have gotten tired of making them and tried to prune them from menus, much to the outrage of our friends.

My grilled pizzas are pretty good, but they are nothing like the gold standard New York pizza that I grew up with. There is a pizzeria 100 yards from Susan's mother's house in Yonkers that makes the classic New York–style pizza. Tony's has ovens that probably came off the boat from Italy in 1950. The place has even burned down twice that I know of, and it keeps coming back. They make a really good pie. Ask them to make it extra crispy, and you are in for a treat.

My grilled pizzas started with Susan's brother, Bobby, one of my favorite foodies. Many of my creations and my favorite cooking instruments have their starts with him. Bobby would come out to Westhampton every summer. He lives in New Hampshire, and one year he stopped at Il Forno's in Rhode Island on the way down. Dinner one night at the beach house centered around Bobby making pizza on the grill.

My pizzas have come a long way from Bobby's inspiration. Over the years, I have tweaked them quite a bit, but they will always have their roots in the night in Westhampton. For me, the key to great pizza is to get the right amount of char on a good crust by using a really hot grill. The downside of a grill is that you can get too much of the heat coming up from the grill. The bottom can be overdone while the top is underdone. Another challenge with making pizza is that it can be tough to keep up with demand while entertaining.

My solution to both of these challenges is to start the pizza on the grill and finish it in the oven on a pizza stone. The result is a really good product that isn't New York pizza but is pretty darn good. Friends in Memphis think it is great, but then again, Memphians like BBQ on their pizza.

A friend from Memphis moved to New Haven, Connecticut. He was telling me how he bragged about my pizza to people in his office in New Haven. I went a little bit crazy, reminding him that New Haven is home to some of the world's best pizza. That being said, my pie is pretty good for Memphis and really good for entertaining.

Kickoff Party Menu
Grilled Pizzas
Margherita
Sausage and Mushroom
Shrimp and Bacon
White/Broccoli
Wild Mushrooms, Caramelized Onion and Gorgonzola
Meat Lovers with Sausage, Meatball and Bacon
Caramelized Leek and Goat Cheese
Roasted Garlic and Fresh Mozzarella
Clam, Bacon and Mozzarella with Fresh Oregano

pizza dough

Ingredients

1¼-ounce packet active dry yeast

1 cup warm water

2¼ cups bread flour

1 teaspoon kosher salt

1 tablespoon olive oil

Extra flour and olive oil for dusting and coating

Cookware Needed

Food processor

Large mixing bowl

Serves 8 People

1. Dissolve the yeast in 1 cup of warm water following the instructions on the yeast package. It takes about 5 minutes for the yeast to fully activate.

2. In the bowl of a food processor fitted with a plastic blade for dough (though I also use the steel blade— both work), pulse flour and salt to combine.

3. With the machine running, add olive oil and yeast/water mixture. Let the processor run for 15 seconds or so until the dough forms into a ball.

4. Generously dust a workspace with flour. Dump the dough ball from the processor onto the floured work area. Dust the ball with more flour, then knead into a well-formed ball.

Step	Prep Time
Dissolve yeast in water	5–6
Pulse together flour and salt	1
Add oil, water and yeast	1
Dust with flour and knead dough ball	3–5
Brush with oil and set in bowl	2–3
Let dough rise 1	45–50
Let dough rise 2	45–50
Let dough rise 3	45–50
Set dough in fridge overnight	480–600
Slack dough out at room temperature	60
Total	**4-12 hrs**

5. Place the ball in a large bowl. Brush on a very thin layer of olive oil, then cover the bowl with plastic wrap. Set aside in a draft-free spot and let dough rise for 45 minutes.

6. When time is up, punch the dough down and reshape into a ball. Repeat 1 or 2 more times.

7. Cut the dough in half. Form into two dough balls and place into an airtight container. Seal it and let it proof overnight in the refrigerator.

8. Before using, bring the dough up to room temperature for 1 hour.

grilled pizza

All of the pizzas have common ingredients and a common process for cooking. They differ in what you put on top. A helpful hint is: Don't go crazy with toppings. The tendency is to put too much on one pizza. The best results come with one or two toppings (three at the most).

Ingredients
1 pizza dough ball
¼ cup olive oil
1½ tablespoons minced garlic
1 cup yellow corn meal
1–2 cups low-moisture mozzarella cheese*
Kosher salt and pepper to taste

Cookware Needed
Food processor
Large mixing bowl

Serves 8 People

1. Preheat your gas grill to as hot as you can get it.

2. Roll out pizza dough until it is ⅜ inch thick. Though I have tried to hand stretch it and throw it the way they do at the pizza places in New York, I get the best results by starting by hand, stretching and pulling the dough to get it roughly shaped then finishing it with a rolling pin (or wine bottle).

3. Cover your pizza peel (a.k.a. paddle) with a thin layer of cornmeal. Place rolled-out pizza dough on top.

4. Place the raw dough on the grill, close the cover and let it cook for a few minutes. When the dough bubbles, check the bottom for doneness. You want it to be slightly charred. Slight char/grill marks are good. Burnt is bad.

5. Take the half-cooked dough off the grill with your peel. Flip the dough so the uncooked side is down. Spoon on a layer of olive oil and minced garlic, brushing it out to thinly coat the cooked side.

6. Prepare each pizza with toppings of your choice.

7. Return pizza to the grill. Cook the bottom until it has good grill/char marks. Take it off the grill and place on a baking tin. (I usually make 3 or 4 pizzas on the grill an hour or so in advance and set them aside to cool.)

8. As the guests begin to arrive, preheat the oven with a pizza stone to 450°F.

9. Finish the pizza in the oven to get them a crispy well done, 5–10 minutes.

*I like the flavor of fresh mozzarella but prefer the performance of low-moisture mozzarella. The problem with fresh mozzarella is the moisture. If you use fresh mozzarella without a few precautions, you will wind up with a soggy pizza. When I use fresh, I cut or shred it, then let it dry out on a paper towel in the refrigerator for an hour or so.

margherita pizza

Ingredients

¾ cup tomato sauce
(from a jar—I use
a simple marinara)

1 cup fresh mozzarella

Basil

Cookware Needed

Gas grill

Rolling pin

Baking sheets

Pizza stone

Pizza peel
(optional, you can
use the bottom of a
baking sheet)

Serves 8 People

1. After you have taken the half-cooked dough off the grill and brushed on olive oil and garlic to thinly coat the cooked side, spoon on and spread a thin layer of tomato sauce.

2. Add a sprinkling (1 cup) of low-moisture mozzarella and top with dots/slices of fresh mozzarella.

3. Sprinkle with kosher salt and freshly ground pepper to taste.

4. After finishing to cook the pizza according to the common process, take it out of the oven and top with fresh basil.

5. Slice and serve.

Step	Prep Time
Roll out pizza dough	5–8 min
Spoon/brush garlic and oil on cooked first side	2–3 min
Add tomato sauce	2–3 min
Add low-moisture and fresh mozzarella	2–3 min
Finish with sprinkling of salt, pepper and fresh herbs	2–3 min
Total	**15-23 min**

Cook Time	Temperature
Grill first side of pizza	Very high for 4–5 min
Grill second side of pizza	Very high for 4–5 min
Finish in oven	450°F for 5–10 min
Total	**13–20 min**

sausage and mushroom pizza

Ingredients

1 pound sweet Italian sausage

1½ cups mushrooms, sliced

5 cloves garlic, sliced thin

½ cup fresh oregano, chopped

Cookware Needed

10 or 12 inch sauté
(or frying) pan

Rolling pin

Gas grill

Baking sheets

Pizza stone

Pizza peel
(optional, you can use
the bottom of a
baking sheet)

Serves 8 People

1. Brown sausage in a sauté pan (can be done hours in advance).

2. After you have taken the half-cooked dough off the grill and brushed on olive oil and garlic to thinly coat the cooked side, add a layer (2 cups) of low-moisture mozzarella.

3. Placed the lightly browned sausage across the pizza.

4. Add a sprinkling of sautéed garlic and fresh mushrooms.

5. Sprinkle with kosher salt and freshly ground pepper to taste.

6. After finishing to cook the pizza according to the common process, take it out of the oven and top with fresh oregano.

7. Slice and serve.

Step	Prep Time
Roll out pizza dough	5–8 min
Slice mushrooms	2–3 min
Spoon/brush garlic and oil on cooked first side	2–3 min
Add layer of mozzarella	2–3 min
Add sausage, mushroom and garlic	2–3 min
Finish with sprinkling of salt, pepper and fresh herbs	2–3 min
Total	15-23 min

Cook Time	Temperature
Sauté garlic	Medium-low for 5–7 min
Brown sausage	Medium-high for 5–10 min
Grill first side of pizza	Very high for 4–5 min
Grill second side of pizza	Very high for 4–5 min
Finish in oven	450°F for 5–10 min
Total	**23–37 min**

shrimp and bacon pizza

Ingredients

1 pound medium-sized
raw shrimp

½ pound bacon,
cut into a ½-inch dice

2 tablespoons capers

½ cup sliced shallots

½ cup fresh Italian parsley

Cookware Needed

10 or 12 inch sauté
(or frying) pan

Rolling pin

Gas grill

Baking sheets

Pizza stone

Pizza peel
(optional, you can use
the bottom of a
baking sheet)

Serves 8 People

1. Lightly sauté shrimp in sauté pan (can be done hours in advance).

2. Lightly sauté bacon in sauté pan (can be done hours in advance).

3. Lightly sauté shallots in sauté pan (can be done hours in advance).

4. After you have taken the half-cooked dough off the grill and brushed on olive oil and garlic to thinly coat the cooked side, add a layer (2 cups) of low-moisture mozzarella.

5. Place shrimp across the pizza.

6. Add a sprinkling of sautéed shallots and bacon.

7. Sprinkle with kosher salt and freshly ground pepper to taste

8. After finishing to cook the pizza according to the common process, take it out of the oven and top with fresh Italian parsley.

9. Slice and serve.

Step	Prep Time
Roll out pizza dough	5–8 min
Slice mushrooms	2–3 min
Spoon/brush garlic and oil on cooked first side	2–3 min
Add layer of mozzarella	2–3 min
Add sausage, mushroom and garlic	2–3 min
Finish with sprinkling of salt, pepper and fresh herbs	2–3 min
Total	**15-23 min**

Cook Time	Temperature
Sauté garlic	Medium-low for 5–7 min
Brown sausage	Medium-high for 5–10 min
Grill first side of pizza	Very high for 4–5 min
Grill second side of pizza	Very high for 4–5 min
Finish in oven	450°F for 5–10 min
Total	**23–37 min**

white/broccoli pizza

Ingredients

2 cups broccoli florets

1½ cups fresh mozzarella

½ cup thinly sliced garlic

½ cup fresh Italian parsley

Cookware Needed

10 or 12 inch sauté
(or frying) pan

Rolling pin

Gas grill

Baking sheets

Pizza stone

Pizza peel
(optional, you can use
the bottom of a
baking sheet)

Serves 8 People

1. Steam broccoli in microwave on high for 3 minutes (can be done hours in advance).

2. Lightly sauté garlic in sauté pan (can be done hours in advance).

3. Lightly sauté shallots in sauté pan (can be done hours in advance)

4. After you have taken the half-cooked dough off the grill and brushed on olive oil and garlic to thinly coat the cooked side, add a layer (1 cup) of low-moisture and fresh mozzarella.

5. Place broccoli across pizza.

6. Add a sprinkling of sautéed garlic.

7. Sprinkle with kosher salt and freshly ground pepper to taste.

8. After finishing to cook the pizza according to the common process, take it out of the oven and top with fresh Italian parsley.

9. Slice and serve.

Step	Prep Time
Prep and slice broccoli, shallots and garlic	2–3 min
Roll out pizza dough	5–8 min
Spoon/brush garlic and oil on cooked first side	2–3 min
Add layer of low-moisture mozzarella	2–3 min
Place pieces of fresh mozzarella	3–4 min
Add shrimp, bacon and shallots	2–3 min
Finish with sprinkling of salt, pepper and fresh herbs	2–3 min
Total	**15-23 min**

Cook Time	Temperature
Microwave broccoli florets	High for 2-3 min
Lightly sauté garlic and shallots	Medium-low for 3-4 min
Grill first side of pizza	Very high for 4–5 min
Grill second side of pizza	Very high for 4–5 min
Finish in oven	450°F for 5–10 min
Total	**18–27 min**

meat lovers pizza with sausage, meatball and bacon

Ingredients

1 pound sweet Italian sausage

1½ cups mushrooms, sliced

5 cloves garlic, sliced thin

½ cup fresh oregano, chopped

Cookware Needed

10 or 12 inch sauté (or frying) pan

Rolling pin

Gas grill

Baking sheets

Pizza stone

Pizza peel (optional, you can use the bottom of a baking sheet)

Serves 8 People

1. Brown sausage in a sauté pan

2. Lightly sauté bacon in sauté pan

3. Lightly sauté shallots in sauté pan (steps 1-3 can be done hours in advance).

4. After you have taken the half-cooked dough off the grill and brushed on olive oil and garlic to thinly coat the cooked side, spread on a layer of tomato sauce.

5. Add a layer (2 cups) of low-moisture mozzarella.

6. Placed the sausage, meatballs and bacon across the pizza.

7. Sprinkle with kosher salt and freshly ground pepper to taste.

8. After finishing to cook the pizza according to the common process, pull it out of the oven and top with basil.

9. Slice and serve.

Cook Time	Temperature
Sauté shallots	Medium-low for 5-7 min
Brown sausage	Medium-high for 5-10 min
Brown bacon	Medium-high for 5-10 min
Grill first side of pizza	Very high for 4–5 min
Grill second side of pizza	Very high for 4–5 min
Finish in oven	450°F for 5–10 min
Total	**28–47 min**

Step	Prep Time
Roll out pizza dough	5–8 min
Slice meatballs	2–3 min
Prep sausage and bacon	3–4 min
Spoon/brush garlic and oil on cooked first side	2–3 min
Spoon on a thin layer of tomato sauce	2–3 min
Add layer of mozzarella	2–3 min
Add sausage, meatballs, bacon and shallots	2–3 min
Finish with sprinkling of salt, pepper and fresh herbs	2–3 min
Total	**15-23 min**

wild mushroom, caramelized onion and gorgonzola pizza

I had the good fortune to work with a world-renowned mushroom expert. Ben Blidjenstien is from Holland, and besides knowing about mushrooms, he is also a true gourmand. If you ask me to list 10 of the top meals I have had in my life, probably five were with Ben. One of the things I learned from Ben was there is a world of flavor beyond simple white mushrooms. Historically, Americans know of one type of mushroom. The white button mushroom, or what the French call a champion, used to be all you could get in the States. Today we have all sorts of options.

This recipe calls for "wild" mushrooms, but I am not suggesting one should go into the local forest to gather them. While my friend Ben could forage up an amazing meal of truly wild mushrooms, my definition of "wild" would include shiitake, chanterelles, porcini or cremini mushrooms. Ben and I were once taking the train from Paris to London and overheard a group of Parisians discussing what is the correct mushroom to serve with chicken. Thirty minutes into the conversation it became clear that consensus was impossible. The point of this story is to challenge you to branch out. There is a world of flavor beyond our white button mushrooms that work really well on pizza.

Ingredients

2 cups mushrooms (shiitake, chanterelles, porcini or cremini work well)

2 cups onions, sliced

2 teaspoons sugar

3 tablespoons butter

½ cup shallots, sliced

1½ cups Gorgonzola cheese, grated

½ cup fresh oregano

1. Slice mushrooms (can be done hours in advance).

2. Sauté onion in butter under medium heat adding 2 teaspoons of sugar to help with the caramelization process (can be done hours in advance).

3. Lightly sauté shallots in sauté pan (can be done hours in advance).

4. After you have taken the half-cooked dough off the grill and brushed on olive oil and garlic

Cookware Needed

10 or 12 inch sauté (or frying) pan

Rolling pin

Gas grill

Baking sheets

Pizza stone

Pizza peel (optional, you can use the bottom of a baking sheet)

Serves 8 People

to thinly coat the cooked side, add a layer (1½ cups) of low-moisture mozzarella.

5. Place mushrooms and caramelized onion across the pizza.

6. Add a sprinkling of Gorgonzola cheese.

7. Sprinkle with kosher salt and freshly ground pepper to taste.

8. After finishing to cook the pizza according to the common process, pull it out of the oven and top with oregano.

9. Slice and serve.

Step	Prep Time
Roll out pizza dough	5–8 min
Slice mushrooms	2–3 min
Prep onion	3–4 min
Prep Gorgonzola	3–4 min
Spoon/brush garlic and oil on cooked first side	2–3 min
Add layer of mozzarella	2–3 min
Add Gorgonzola, mushrooms and shallots	4–5 min
Finish with sprinkling of salt, pepper and fresh herbs	2–3 min
Total	**15-23 min**

Cook Time	Temperature
Sauté onion	Medium for 8-12 min
Grill first side of pizza	Very high for 4–5 min
Grill second side of pizza	Very high for 4–5 min
Finish in oven	450°F for 5–10 min
Total	**21–32 min**

caramelized leek and goat cheese pizza

Ingredients

2 cups leeks

2 teaspoons sugar

3 tablespoons butter

1½ cups goat cheese, cut into ¼-inch slices (or quarter-sized pieces)

½ cup fresh basil

Cookware Needed

10 or 12 inch sauté (or frying) pan

Rolling pin

Gas grill

Baking sheets

Pizza stone

Pizza peel (optional, you can use the bottom of a baking sheet)

Serves 8 People

1. Sauté onion in butter under medium heat, adding 2 tablespoons of sugar to help with the caramelization process (can be done hours in advance).

2. Lightly sauté leeks in sauté pan (can be done hours in advance).

3. After you have taken the half-cooked dough off the grill and brushed on olive oil and garlic to thinly coat the cooked side, add a layer (1½ cups) of low-moisture mozzarella.

4. Place sautéed leeks across the pizza.

5. Add slices/dots of goat cheese across the pizza.

6. Sprinkle with kosher salt and freshly ground pepper to taste.

7. After finishing to cook the pizza according to the common process, pull it out of the oven and top with basil.

8. Slice and serve.

Step	Prep Time
Roll out pizza dough	5–8 min
Prep leeks	3–4min
Prep goat cheese	3–4 min
Spoon/brush garlic and oil on cooked first side	2–3 min
Add layer of mozzarella	2–3 min
Add goat cheeses and leeks	4–5 min
Finish with sprinkling of salt, pepper and fresh herbs	2–3 min
Total	**15-23 min**

Cook Time	Temperature
Sauté leeks	Medium for 8-12 min
Grill first side of pizza	Very high for 4–5 min
Grill second side of pizza	Very high for 4–5 min
Finish in oven	450°F for 5–10 min
Total	**23–32 min**

roasted garlic and fresh mozzarella pizza

Ingredients

2 heads garlic (about 10–15 cloves)

2 tablespoons olive oil

Salt and pepper

1½ cups fresh mozzarella

½ cup fresh basil, chopped

Cookware Needed

10 or 12 inch sauté (or frying) pan

Rolling pin

Gas grill

Baking sheets

Pizza stone

Pizza peel (optional, you can use the bottom of a baking sheet)

Serves 8 People

1. Preheat oven to 390°F.

2. Slice of the tip of the head of garlic, just exposing the raw cloves. Brush with olive oil and sprinkle with salt and pepper. Wrap the garlic heads in aluminum foil and bake for 50 minutes.

3. Allow garlic to cool, then squeeze cloves out of the head of garlic.

4. After you have taken the half-cooked dough off the grill and brushed on olive oil to thinly coat the cooked side, add a sprinkling (1½ cups) of low-moisture mozzarella and top with dots or slices of fresh mozzarella.

5. Place roasted garlic pieces across the pizza.

6. Sprinkle with kosher salt and freshly ground pepper to taste.

7. After finishing to cook the pizza according to the common process, pull it out of the oven and top with basil.

8. Slice and serve.

Step	Prep Time
Roll out pizza dough	5–8 min
Prep garlic heads for roasting	3–4 min
Squeeze out roasted garlic	3–4 min
Prep fresh mozzarella	4–5 min
Spoon/brush garlic and oil on cooked first side	2–3 min
Add layer of mozzarella	2–3 min
Add fresh mozzarella and roasted garlic	4–5 min
Finish with sprinkling of salt, pepper and fresh herbs	2–3 min
Total	**15-23 min**

Cook Time	Temperature
Roast garlic	390°F for 45–60 min
Grill first side of pizza	Very high for 4–5 min
Grill second side of pizza	Very high for 4–5 min
Finish in oven	450°F for 5–10 min
Total	**58-80 min**

clam, bacon and fresh mozzarella pizza

Ingredients

1½ cups fresh mozzarella

1 8-ounce can chopped clams

½ pound bacon,
cut in ½-inch slices

½ cup shallots, sliced

½ cup fresh oregano, chopped

Cookware Needed

10 or 12 inch sauté
(or frying) pan

Rolling pin

Gas grill

Baking sheets

Pizza stone

Pizza peel
(optional, you can use the
bottom of a baking sheet)

Serves 8 People

1. Lightly sauté bacon in sauté pan (can be done hours in advance).

2. Lightly sauté shallots in sauté pan (can be done hours in advance).

3. After you have taken the half-cooked dough off the grill and brushed on olive oil and garlic to thinly coat the cooked side, add a sprinkling (1½ cups) of low-moisture mozzarella and top with dots or slices of fresh mozzarella.

4. Place clams, bacon and shallot across the pizza.

5. Sprinkle with kosher salt and freshly ground pepper to taste.

6. After finishing to cook the pizza according to the common process, pull it out of the oven and top with oregano.

7. Slice and serve.

Step	Prep Time
Roll out pizza dough	5–8 min
Slice mushrooms	2–3 min
Spoon/brush garlic and oil on cooked first side	2–3 min
Add layer of mozzarella	2–3 min
Add pieces of fresh mozzarella	3–4 min
Add clams, bacon and shallots	2–3 min
Finish with sprinkling of salt, pepper and fresh herbs	2–3 min
Total	**15-23 min**

Cook Time	Temperature
Sauté shallots	Medium-low for 5–7 min
Grill first side of pizza	Very high for 4–5 min
Grill second side of pizza	Very high for 4–5 min
Finish in oven	450°F for 5–10 min
Total	**18-27 min**

Anecdotes

By now you have probably figured out that I like my pizza crispy. I can't say if it is my New York upbringing or the fact that Memphians like their pizza half cooked. I once asked the owner of a pizza place in Memphis why he half cooked his pizza. The guy was from Italy and had lived in NJ. He told me, "If I cooked pizza the way I liked, I wouldn't sell a single pie in Memphis. Memphians like their pizza 'white' or basically raw." The flip to this is that my Memphis friends rave about my grilled pizzas. I guess it is because the grilled pizzas are so different from what they grew up with that they fall into a different category.

I have found that one of the challenges of living in Middle America is that the consumer likes things "mild," be it pizza, bread, coffee or whatever there is. The average American consumer has historically been opposed to stronger flavors. This is definitely changing. More Americans are being exposed to authentic cuisines with stronger flavors. The fact is that as baby boomers age, their taste buds weaken. So what was once considered too spicy might not be so bad now.

Prep Schedule—Mise en Place (for a Saturday evening dinner)

Thursday*

Prep and sauté:

Bacon, sausage, garlic, shallots, shrimp, caramelized onion and leeks, mushroom, broccoli, fresh mozzarella, goat cheese, olive oil and garlic

Saturday

3:00 PM	Grill and assemble pizzas
7:00	Bake pizza 1
7:10	Guests arrive, serve wine
7:15	Chit chat, serve pizza 1
7:30	Bake pizza 2
7:40	Serve pizza 2
7:50	Bake pizza 3
8:00	Serve pizza 3
8:10	Bake pizza 4
8:20	Serve pizza 4

* The prep/precook work can be done hours or up to 2 days in advance.

Wine Recommendations

Wine	Origin	Composition	Price
Red			
Rutherford Cabernet Sauvignon	Napa, CA	Cabernet Sauvignon	$25.00
Grochau Cellars Pinot Noir	Dundee Hills ,OR	Pinot Noir	$35.00
Walter Scott La Combe Verte	Paso Robles, CA	Red Blend	$20.00
White			
Louis LaTour Chardonnay	Burgundy, France	Chardonnay	$20.00
Robert Mondavi Chardonnay	Napa Valley, CA	Chardonnay	$17.99
Atemms Pinot Grigio Ramato	Venezia Giulia, Italia	Pinot Grigio	$12.25

ABOUT THE AUTHOR

Paul Kenny grew up primarily in suburban New York. His dad was a college dean at Pace University and his mom taught junior high and then college mathematics. His dad had a doctorate in rhetoric and his mother had a masters in mathematics. With this "right brain – left brain conflict" in his genetics the author's biggest complaint was that "while brains ran in the family it was unfair that when it came to him they walked".

After finishing business school he started his career with General Foods Corporation in White Plains New York and married the love of his life Susan Herbert Kenny. Life as a corporate nomad started with 5 years in New York then moved him to California, then to Delaware and finally to Memphis Tennessee. It was sort of like right coast, left coast, right coast and then the middle of America. Through these moving years his daughter Jennifer was born in California and then son Brian was born in Delaware. Susan decided that moving was fine for two, but she wanted her children growing up in one place. Hence what was planned to be a six month stint in Memphis has led to over 25 years and counting.

This personal and career background has been a perfect lead into Supper Clubs. His parents loved to entertain at dinner parties and moving quite often led to using socializing over a meal as a way to meet new friends in new places. Hence, Paul and Susan have been in all types of supper clubs for over 30 years. There have been big clubs, small clubs and everything in between. Along the way they have had a lot of great meals, made a lot of mistakes, but most importantly made many great friends.

Paul's career in the food business has also been a cornerstone. As General Foods morphed into to Kraft Foods his career settled into over 20 years with Kraft Food Ingredients. KFI was a small company within Kraft focused on food ingredients. This small company within a large company allowed the author to have stints in finance, sales, marketing and operations in both domestic and international markets. The author led the marketing team at KFI for years. Technology was a key competitive advantage for KFI and the marketing and sales team used Culinary as a way to explain that advantage. This allowed the author to work with a great team of chefs, travel the world, experience great cuisines and then bring ideas back to his neighborhood supper club.

Everyone likes to socialize over a meal especially the author. Whether you are using Supper Clubs to make new friends or getting together with old friends, good food along with good wine leads to good times.

Morgan James
Speakers Group

www.TheMorganJamesSpeakersGroup.com

We connect Morgan James published authors with live and online events and audiences who will benefit from their expertise.

Morgan James makes all of our titles available
through the Library for All Charity Organization.

www.LibraryForAll.org

CPSIA information can be obtained
at www.ICGtesting.com
Printed in the USA
JSHW052237280322
24345JS00001B/140

9 781683 505044